THE FIRST WORLD WAR

Andrew Wrenn

CAMBRIDGE
UNIVERSITY PRESS

PUBLISHED BY THE PRESS SYNDICATE OF THE UNIVERSITY OF CAMBRIDGE
The Pitt Building, Trumpington Street, Cambridge CB2 1RP, United Kingdom

CAMBRIDGE UNIVERSITY PRESS
The Edinburgh Building, Cambridge CB2 2RU, United Kingdom
40 West 20th Street, New York, NY 10011-4211, USA
10 Stamford Road, Oakleigh, Melbourne 3166, Australia

First published 1997

Printed in the United Kingdom at the University Press, Cambridge

Typeset in Monotype Octavian and FF Meta

A catalogue record for this book is available from the British Library

ISBN 0 521 57775 6 paperback

Produced by Gecko Limited, Bicester, Oxon

Illustrations by Robert Calow, Martin Sanders and Gecko Limited, Bicester, Oxon

Acknowledgements
Cover: 'Are you in this?', Imperial War Museum, London.
AKG London: 34*b*; Canadian War Museum, Ottowa, Canada/Bridgeman Art Library, London: 44*t*;
Imperial War Museum, London/Bridgeman: 43*r*, 60, Private Collection/Bridgeman: 22*l*; Getty Images: 4, 5,
16*b*, 17, 22*r*, 24, 27, 28, 34–35 *background*, 45*b*, 50, 56; Michael Holford: 18*l*; Imperial War Museum, London:
16*t*, 29*r*, 35*t* and *b*, 51*r*, 61; Peter Newark's Military Pictures: 8, 10, 15, 16*m*, 20*r*, 23*r*, 26, 37, 38*l* and *r*, 43*tl*, 45*tl*,
47 *background*, 49*t* and *b*, 51*l*, 54*r*, 63 *background*; Pictorial Nostalgia: 18*r*; Popperfoto: 13, 19, 20*l*, 23*l*, 25*t*, 31,
32, 45*tr*, 54 *background*; Reproduced with permission of Punch Limited: 21, 29*l*, 43*bl*; Topham Picturepoint: 6, 9,
25*b*, 30, 33, 39, 42, 44*b*, 46, 52, 55; Ullstein Bilderdienst: 36.

Picture research by Sandie Huskinson-Rolfe of PHOTOSEEKERS

Contents

Origins of the First World War

On 4 August 1914, German soldiers invaded Belgium. The First World War had begun. Soon many of the most powerful countries in Europe were at war.

The system of alliances in Europe, and the arms race between the largest European countries, had helped to create the international tensions that had led to the outbreak of the war.

The opposing alliances

In the ten years before the outbreak of the war, there were two rival alliances of great powers in Europe. The Triple Entente consisted of France, Britain and Russia. The Central Powers (also known as the Triple Alliance) consisted of Germany, Austria-Hungary and Italy.

EUROPE 1914 – THE RIVAL ALLIANCES

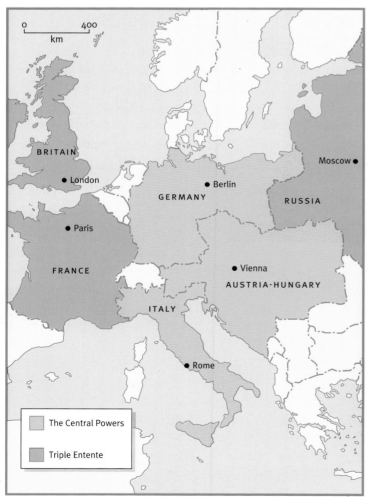

While Germany itself was strong, its allies were not. Austria-Hungary was a huge, rickety empire made up of 11 quarrelling nations. Some, such as the Czechs, wanted independence, while others, for example the Serbs, wanted union with neighbouring states. Germany's other ally, Italy, was unreliable, and it was desperate to remain neutral in any coming war.

There was long-standing hostility between France and Germany. Germany had become a united country in 1871, when it defeated France in the Franco-Prussian War and took the territory of Alsace-Lorraine from the French. Germany expected France to launch a war of revenge to regain Alsace-Lorraine. Germany also felt threatened and surrounded by the members of the Triple Entente, with France and Britain to the west, and Russia to the east.

The arms race

By 1914, Germany was one of the greatest powers in Europe. It was ruled by the German emperor Kaiser Wilhelm II. He controlled a navy of 97 battleships that challenged Britain's control of the sea, and his army of 2.2 million men was the best-trained and best-equipped in the world.

Kaiser Wilhelm II with Von Moltke behind him on manoeuvres before the First World War.

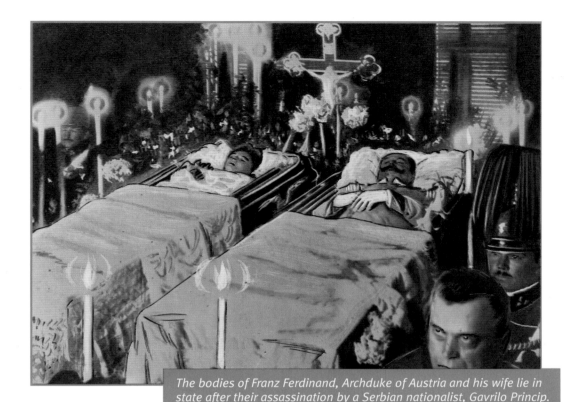

The bodies of Franz Ferdinand, Archduke of Austria and his wife lie in state after their assassination by a Serbian nationalist, Gavrilo Princip.

In spite of the arrogant over-confidence of the Kaiser, the Germans were afraid of fighting a war on two fronts – in the east and in the west.

The Germans particularly feared the huge Russian army. The 'Russian steamroller' had millions of peasants to call on, and it was believed to be improving all the time. Some historians think that Germany started the First World War in 1914 deliberately, because the German government thought that the Russian army would be fully modernised by 1917, and it wanted to defeat Russia before this could happen.

Military planning

If it was to win a war in Europe, Germany would need to win a swift and decisive victory in the west. The German general Count Alfred von Schlieffen drew up a plan to defeat France within six weeks before the 'Russian steamroller' could be mobilised (in position and ready to fight).

The victorious German troops could then be transported across Germany by train to face the Russian onslaught. In the minds of many Germans, the final struggle for the mastery of Europe would be between the Teutonic (German) race and the Slav (Russian and some eastern European) races.

Assassination

On 28 June 1914, the heir to the throne of Austria-Hungary was shot dead in Sarajevo in the Balkans by a Serbian nationalist. This was because there was a dispute between Austria-Hungary and Serbia about who should rule over the Serbs of Bosnia.

Austria-Hungary decided to go to war against Serbia. Because of the system of European alliances, this conflict drew in several other countries. Serbia was allied with Russia. Germany was ready to fight alongside Austria-Hungary. Russia was prepared to go to war in support of Serbia. France and Britain decided to support Russia. Italy remained neutral in 1914.

Thus all the most powerful countries of Europe went to war, with Germany and its allies on one side, and the Allies (Britain, France and Russia, and the other countries that fought on their side) on the other.

Discussion points

> Why did people in Britain feel threatened by Germany in the years before 1914?

> Why did the German government fear a war on two fronts? How did it plan to avoid this possibility?

The two plans

German hopes of a quick victory in the war were based on the Schlieffen Plan. The French had different ideas: their army intended to smash the German forces by following Plan XVII.

The Schlieffen Plan

The Schlieffen Plan covered what the Germans thought would be the first three phases of the war.

Count Alfred von Schlieffen, Chief of the General Staff of the German Army and author of the Schlieffen Plan.

THE SCHLIEFFEN PLAN

(1) Germany had one of the finest railway systems in the world. This would be used to transport troops to the front line.

(2) Invade through neutral Belgium with overwhelming force. Make the troops crossing the central and northern parts of Belgium eight times stronger than the forces invading through the wooded hills of the Ardennes region. Germany would then have enough troops to attack west of Paris.

(3) Within six weeks, German troops would have encircled the city of Paris from the west and east, forcing its surrender. The French would then make peace. German troops could then be transported by rail to face 'the Russian steamroller'.

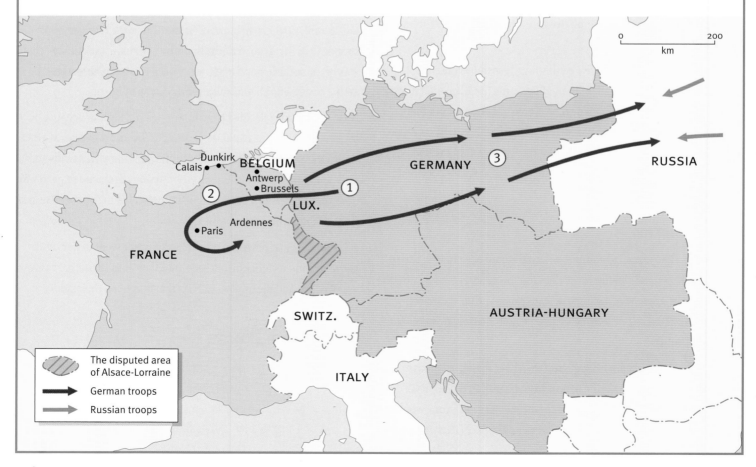

The disputed area of Alsace-Lorraine

German troops

Russian troops

PHASE 1: WAR WITH FRANCE, AND THE ALSACE-LORRAINE BORDER

> Germany knew that it did not have the strength to fight both Russia and France at the same time. Germany estimated that it would take Russia six weeks to mobilise its troops. This would give Germany time to defeat France quickly.

> The French border with the German-held Alsace-Lorraine was protected by mountains and a string of ten French forts. It would thus be difficult for Germany to invade France by this route.

> Italian troops would help Germany to defend the Alsace-Lorraine frontier against any French attack.

PHASE 2: THE GERMAN INVASION OF FRANCE THROUGH BELGIUM

> Germany knew that the Belgian army was badly equipped and poorly trained. The Germans guessed that the Belgians would not fight. A German general commented: 'We could allow them to line the roads and watch us as we advance.'

> Germany thought that the British would probably remain neutral if war broke out between France and Germany.

> If Britain did fight, the Germans believed that its forces would arrive too late to help the French. The German Kaiser later described the British Expeditionary Force (the British troops) as 'that contemptible little army'.

> The Germans believed that international opinion, including that in Britain, would ignore the treaty of 1839 that had declared Belgium to be neutral. The Kaiser later described the treaty as 'a scrap of paper'.

PHASE 3: THE GERMAN DEFEAT OF FRANCE

> Germany assumed that the French would make peace if the Germans captured Paris.

> German troops could then be transported by rail to face the 'Russian steamroller'.

> Germany thought that Britain would allow a hostile foreign army to occupy the important Channel ports of Ostend, Dunkirk, Boulogne and Calais, even though Calais was only 22 miles away from the key British port of Dover.

The French reply: Plan XVII

By 1913, the French had learned of the outline of the Schlieffen Plan from their spies. However, they made no plans to halt any German advance through Belgium, as they did not think that they could stop the Germans there. Instead, the French general Joseph Joffre planned a massive offensive on the German frontier in northern Alsace-Lorraine. His plan was called Plan XVII.

The French military believed that the élan (the flair and fighting spirit) of their army would lead to victory. A leading French general, Ferdinand Foch, spoke of an *offensive à outrance* (an offensive to the limit). In this type of offensive, in order to win, you had to always attack, and never retreat. To retreat, or to let the enemy attack you, was considered rank cowardice.

The aim of Plan XVII was that the French offensive would push the Germans back from the border. France would then free Alsace-Lorraine before pushing on to Berlin, the German capital. Unknown to the Germans, the British and French had been drawing up secret plans for military cooperation since 1911. British officers and generals were also enthusiastic about the planned offensives and the potential impact of French military élan.

Discussion point

> What weaknesses were there in the Schlieffen Plan and in Plan XVII?

Failure of the Schlieffen Plan

The Schlieffen Plan did not work. The German government blamed its leading general, Count Helmuth von Moltke, for this. In September 1914, it replaced him as German commander in the west with General Erich von Falkenhayn. Historians have argued about the reasons for the failure of the Schlieffen Plan ever since.

Was the failure of the plan the fault of Moltke?

The Schlieffen Plan failed in three stages.

SOURCE A

The Germans advancing, painted by Anton Hoffman in 1914.

STAGE 1
AUGUST 1914: BELGIAN RESISTANCE, BRITISH INVOLVEMENT AND RUSSIAN MOBILISATION

> In August, Germany invaded Belgium. Britain stood by its 1839 guarantee of Belgium's neutrality and declared war on Germany on 4 August. Within a week, 120,000 troops of the British Expeditionary Force had been secretly shipped to France.

> The Belgian army resisted the German invasion. It held up the German advance, particularly in fortress cities such as Liège. Despite this, Belgium's capital city of Brussels fell on 20 August.

> Russia mobilised its forces much more quickly than Germany had expected, and it invaded Germany on 17 August. The German commander Moltke was forced to transfer troops from Belgium to the east to fight the Russians.

> Meanwhile, the French counter-attack, Plan XVII, failed completely. The French, under Joffre, were unable to break through the German defences at the Alsace-Lorraine border, and there were 300,000 French casualties.

THE SCHLIEFFEN PLAN FAILS: THE BELGIAN RESPONSE

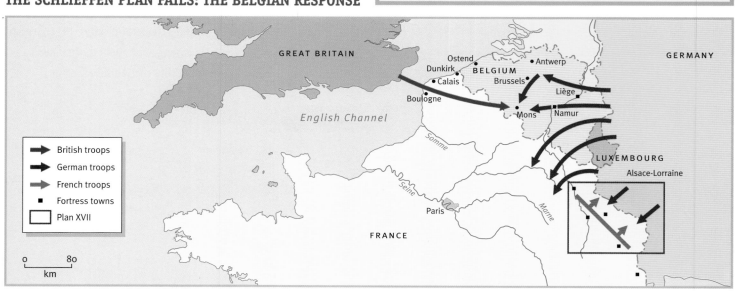

Legend:
- British troops
- German troops
- French troops
- Fortress towns
- Plan XVII

0   80
km

STAGE 2
AUGUST–SEPTEMBER 1914: THE BATTLE OF THE MARNE

> The German advance across Belgium was held up briefly by the British Expeditionary Force at Mons on 23 August. The British then retreated south to join the French.

> The Germans marched into France, but they were forced, because of their lack of soldiers, to sweep east of Paris, rather than west, and they failed to encircle the city.

> The French armies retreating from the German forces were reinforced by the French troops who had failed to take Alsace-Lorraine under Plan XVII.

> General Joffre inspired the French armies to resist the German advance, and he rushed reserve troops to the front from Paris, using taxis when necessary. He ordered that 'a unit which can no longer advance must at all costs retain the ground it has gained and rather than retire, be killed on the spot'.

> Over the four days of 5–9 September, at the Battle of the Marne, the exhausted Germans were thrown back from the Marne river. They began to dig trenches to defend themselves.

> Isolated from the battle in his Luxembourg headquarters, Moltke lost control of his armies and despaired. The German Crown Prince called him 'a broken man literally struggling to hold back his tears as he called for a general retreat'. The German casualty figures were so high that they were never published.

THE SCHLIEFFEN PLAN FAILS: THE BATTLE OF THE MARNE

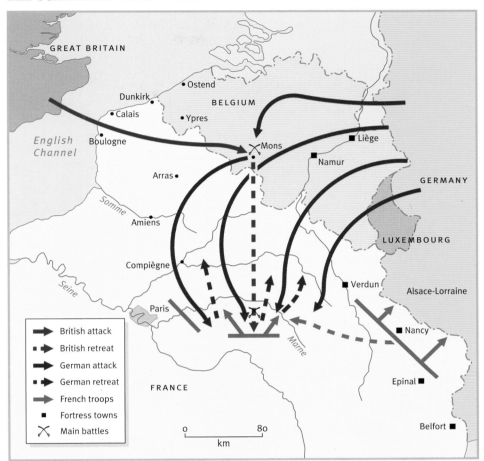

Legend:
- British attack
- British retreat
- German attack
- German retreat
- French troops
- ■ Fortress towns
- ✕ Main battles

0 ——— 80 km

SOURCE B

French soldiers being mobilised for the Battle of the Marne using various forms of transport, including 600 Paris taxis.

SOURCE C

A French regiment parades the colours before the Battle of the Marne. Painted by Georges Scott in 1915.

THE RACE FOR THE SEA

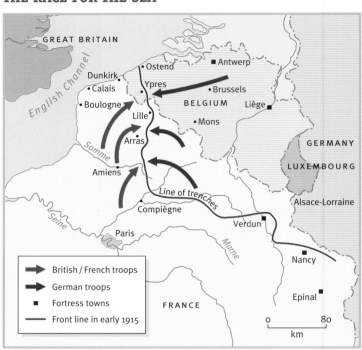

Legend:
→ British / French troops
➡ German troops
■ Fortress towns
— Front line in early 1915

0 — 80 km

SOURCE D

A historian explains how trench warfare began.

On 14 September ... the Germans ... were exhausted, could march no more; they ... scratched holes in the ground, set up machine guns. To everyone's amazement, the advancing Allies hesitated, stopped... One man with a machine gun, protected by mounds of earth, was more powerful than advancing masses. Trench warfare had begun. The war of movement ended when men dug themselves in.

A. J. P. Taylor, *The First World War*, 1963

STAGE 3
OCTOBER 1914: THE RACE FOR THE SEA

> By October 1914, the Germans had failed to capture Paris, and they had been stopped at the Battle of the Marne. Both sides now rushed troops north to capture the Channel ports in the 'race for the sea'.

> On 8 October, the Germans took Ostend, and on 15 October they captured Antwerp, despite the reinforcements of British marines rushed to its defence by the British government minister Winston Churchill.

> On 18 October, Ypres in Belgium was recaptured from the Germans, and the other Channel ports were safe in Allied hands.

> The race for the sea was over. Both sides 'dug in' for the winter in a line of trenches 470 kilometres long, stretching from the North Sea to the French–Swiss border.

>> Activities

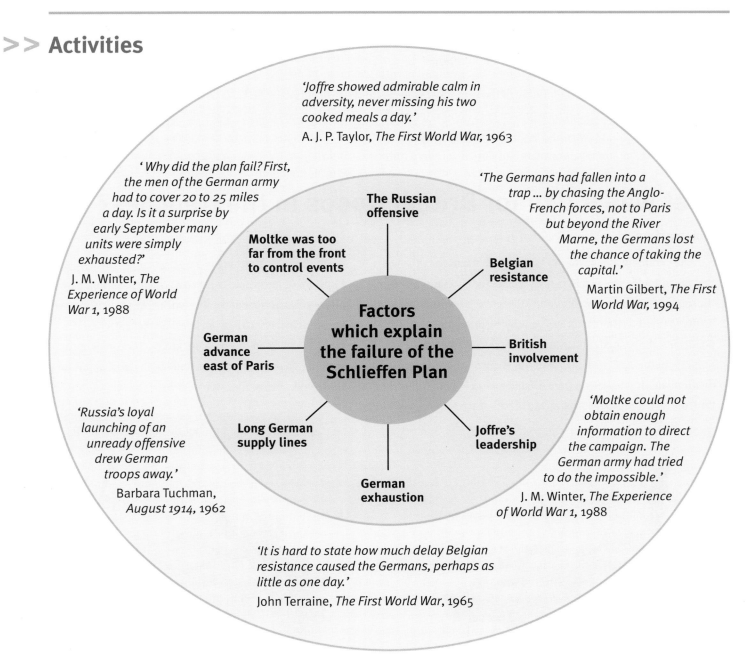

'Joffre showed admirable calm in adversity, never missing his two cooked meals a day.'
A. J. P. Taylor, *The First World War*, 1963

' Why did the plan fail? First, the men of the German army had to cover 20 to 25 miles a day. Is it a surprise by early September many units were simply exhausted?'
J. M. Winter, *The Experience of World War 1*, 1988

'The Germans had fallen into a trap ... by chasing the Anglo-French forces, not to Paris but beyond the River Marne, the Germans lost the chance of taking the capital.'
Martin Gilbert, *The First World War*, 1994

'Russia's loyal launching of an unready offensive drew German troops away.'
Barbara Tuchman, *August 1914*, 1962

'Moltke could not obtain enough information to direct the campaign. The German army had tried to do the impossible.'
J. M. Winter, *The Experience of World War 1*, 1988

'It is hard to state how much delay Belgian resistance caused the Germans, perhaps as little as one day.'
John Terraine, *The First World War*, 1965

The Russian offensive

Moltke was too far from the front to control events

Belgian resistance

German advance east of Paris

British involvement

Long German supply lines

Joffre's leadership

German exhaustion

Factors which explain the failure of the Schlieffen Plan

1 The inner ring of the diagram shows the factors that contributed to the failure of the Schlieffen Plan. Match these factors up with the correct quotes in the outer circle.

2 List the factors in the inner ring in order of their importance as explanations for the failure of the Schlieffen Plan. For example, if you think that the most important factor was Belgian resistance, put that at the top of your list.

3 How many of these factors did Moltke have control over? Is it fair to blame him for the plan's failure?

4 Why was the war not over by Christmas 1914?

The Western Front

At the beginning of the war, most generals and politicians expected it to be a short war of fast military movements dominated by the cavalry (mounted troops). They thought that there would be a swift victory for the winning side. The reality of life on the Western Front after the armies had dug in was very different.

What was it like for British troops in the trenches?

Trench warfare

A cavalry training manual of 1907 stated that 'it must be expected that the rifle, effective as it is, cannot replace the effect produced by the speed of the horse, the charge and the terror of cold steel'. The reality of trench warfare took everyone by surprise, including the politicians, the generals and, not least, the soldiers themselves. From the autumn of 1914, the Allies (the British and the French) and the Germans dug in along a front 470 kilometres long that stretched from the North Sea to the Alps on the French–Swiss border.

All the trenches were dug in a zigzag to make them a more difficult target for gunners, and to prevent a shell blast from blowing away all the soldiers right down the trench. The soldiers were supposed to spend eight days in the front line, and then be relieved by replacement troops brought up through the communications trenches. In practice, soldiers could be in the front line for two or three weeks before they were relieved.

A cross-section of a typical British regulation trench.

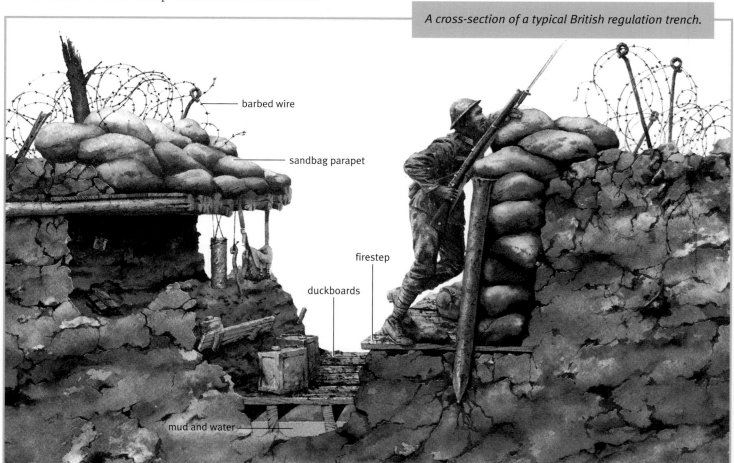

barbed wire

sandbag parapet

firestep

duckboards

mud and water

The living conditions

All soldiers were infested with lice. These were very small, transparent insect parasites that fed on blood up to 12 times a day. The British soldiers called them 'chats', and the only way they could get rid of them was either to crack them off with a fingernail, or to burn them out of the seams of clothing with a candle flame. This process took hours, and it became a great social occasion, called 'chatting'.

In winter, one of the greatest enemies was the weather. The soldiers wore extra underclothes or even layers of newspapers, but the cold still seeped through. In 1917, 21,000 British soldiers were admitted to hospital with frostbite, but the army refused to take frostbite seriously, and treated the soldiers as if they had committed a crime.

The trenches were often full of mud and water from constant rain. The huge artillery (gun) bombardments of both sides churned up the mud and destroyed the trench drainage systems. During the Battle of Passchendaele in the autumn of 1917, thousands of men drowned in the mud, and whole gun and mule teams disappeared without trace.

The rain and mud also made it harder to get supplies into the front line, and so there was only enough to eat when the weather was good or when there had been many casualties. Some soldiers suffered from 'trench foot' when their feet became infected from standing in water and mud. This often led to gangrene, which meant that the foot had to be amputated.

The conditions in summer could be just as bad. The warmth increased the stench of the latrines and decaying dead bodies. Behind the lines, each division of troops had 6,000 horses that produced 40 tonnes of manure a day.

SOURCE A

An outpost in front of the Allied lines, near Ypres.

The daily routine

In contrast to the popular image of heroic warfare, life for the soldiers in the front-line trenches was either horrific or extremely dull. Half an hour before dawn, all the men had to 'stand to'. This meant standing on the firestep with their rifle ready in case of an enemy attack that hardly ever came. The men slept either in dugouts or in 'funk holes' carved out of the side of a trench. After stand-to, one sentry per platoon, or squad, of soldiers was left on duty on the firestep. Breakfast might consist of army biscuit, which was sometimes hard enough to break a soldier's teeth, one loaf divided between three men, jam, and a mug of tea with no milk.

During the day, the sergeant of each platoon organised duties for his men. Some did sentry duty on the firestep. The concentration that this required was exhausting. Some men went to collect rations (food allowances) and supplies from the support trenches. Water was brought back in cans that had been used for petrol, and so it stank of fuel. Some of the men were allowed to 'rest'. In fact, this meant repairing the trenches, replacing barbed wire and duckboards, and filling sandbags. The whole platoon 'stood down' at dusk, and their only comfort was an issue of strong rum.

Action

Much of the activity of trench life only began at night. Soldiers were posted on sentry duty, which meant hours of staring out into the darkness of 'no-man's land' (the unoccupied land between the two front lines). Others might volunteer to go out into no-man's land to a listening post, perhaps a shell hole, near the enemy front line where they could overhear German voices.

Sometimes, information would be gathered by a night patrol or through a full-scale raid on an enemy trench. Star shells were fired by both sides to burst over no-man's land and reveal any activity or troop movements by the enemy.

Over the top

The boredom of trench life was relieved only by battles. Each side was normally warned of a coming enemy attack by a preliminary bombardment of its front line. After several days, the infantry (the foot soldiers) of the attacking side would be sent 'over the top' of their trenches into no-man's land to charge the enemy front line. Each soldier would be carrying a rifle with a fixed bayonet, and he would be weighed down by over 27 kg of equipment. Often, soldiers were caught in barbed wire, and mown down by enemy machine gunners before they could get across no-man's land.

Shrapnel shells were often used as the ammunition in field guns. These were shells that were filled with steel ball bearings, and they burst before hitting the ground, spraying their contents in a 200 metres by 30 metres cone. Most deaths were not caused by hand-to-hand fighting, but by flying debris from shells. Mud would then get into the wounds, and turn them septic.

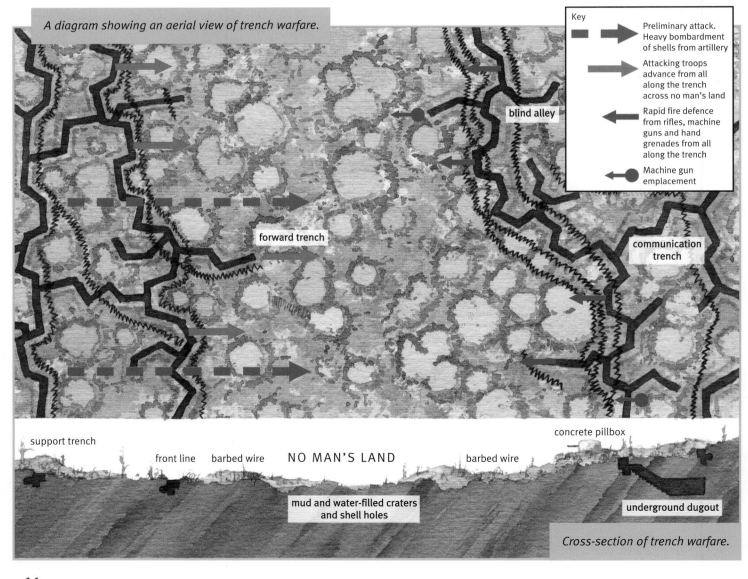

A diagram showing an aerial view of trench warfare.

Key

Preliminary attack. Heavy bombardment of shells from artillery

Attacking troops advance from all along the trench across no man's land

Rapid fire defence from rifles, machine guns and hand grenades from all along the trench

Machine gun emplacement

blind alley

communication trench

forward trench

support trench

front line   barbed wire   NO MAN'S LAND   barbed wire

concrete pillbox

mud and water-filled craters and shell holes

underground dugout

Cross-section of trench warfare.

What can we learn from the following five sources about the conditions faced by soldiers on the Western Front?

SOURCE B

Sydney Booth, a soldier who was there, described what it was like to go 'over the top'.

We saw it, we saw men hanging on the wire, some screaming 'shoot me, do me in'. The longer they hung on the wire, the more they attracted the bullets. It was terrible.

John Giles, *The Somme Then and Now,* 1986

SOURCE C

French casualties in a trench at Argonne in 1915.

SOURCE D

C. E. Carrington, another British veteran, described the fighting.

As we moved forward a sniper fired almost from behind us. I felt the bullet crack in my ear and Corporal Matthews who was walking beside me, fell dead in the twinkling of an eye. He was alive and then he was dead and there was nothing human left in him. He fell with a neat round hole in his forehead and the back of his head blown out.

John Giles, *The Somme Then and Now,* 1986

SOURCE E

Graham Seton Hutchison explained how, in the heat of battle, the ordinary rules of war were sometimes forgotten.

'Fix Bayonets'. Once more my lads rose from the blood-soaked fields in a mad rush. I had turned beast. I was murderer, breath coming in short gasps, teeth set, hands clenched round my rifle, nerves and sinews tense with life. 'An eye for an eye, a tooth for a tooth.' Four German soldiers raised their arms in surrender. I could hear the breath of the sergeant coming in deep snarls beside me. I crashed through the undergrowth, bayonet and rifle levelled to the charge, my great weight and strength gathered behind the thrust. A man crumpled before my bayonet. The sergeant pierced another as a knife goes through butter. A soldier with a cry turned to run. I thrust my bayonet. The man stumbled and fell, his weight dragging the rifle from the hand of his slayer.

John Giles, *The Somme Then and Now,* 1986

SOURCE F

Soldiers wounded in no-man's land sometimes died from drowning in mud or in shell holes filled with water. Rescuing the wounded was very dangerous. The British poet Robert Graves, who was an officer in the First World War, described one wounded man's death.

Samson lay groaning, about twenty yards beyond the front trench. Several attempts were made to rescue him. He had been very badly hit. Three men got killed in three attempts ... In the end his own orderly managed to crawl out to him. Samson waved him back saying he was riddled through and not worth rescuing; he sent his apologies to the Company for making such a noise ... At dusk we all went out to get the wounded, leaving only sentries in the line. The first dead body I came upon was Samson's, hit in seventeen places. I found that he had forced his knuckles into his mouth to stop himself crying out and attracting any more men to their death.

Robert Graves, *Goodbye to All That,* 1929

SOURCE G

Gassed, *by J.S. Sargent.*

Gas attacks

The Germans first released poisonous gas on 22 April 1915 at Langemarck, near Ypres in Belgium. Three types of gas were used in the war:

> Chlorine gas caused its victims to drown in the water produced in their own lungs.

> Phosgene gas was 18 times more powerful than chlorine gas, hard to smell, and impossible to see. It took its victims 48 hours to die, coughing up litres of yellow froth from their lungs.

> Mustard gas burned exposed skin, sometimes to the bone, and it could burn out lungs.

SOURCE H

British machine gunners on the Western Front in 1916 wearing gas masks.

SOURCE I

Blinded British troops, victims of a gas attack, line up for treatment.

If the wind changed direction during a gas attack, the gas could drift back and kill soldiers on the side that had released this terrible weapon of war. Eventually, gas masks were developed to protect soldiers during gas attacks.

SOURCE J

A tank crossing British trenches in 1917.

The development of the tank

Governments on both sides of the war were constantly searching for new methods of breaking the stalemate, or deadlock, and ending the human slaughter. Winston Churchill promoted the idea of using armoured machines driven on caterpillar tracks, which were devised by enthusiasts working in the agricultural-machinery industry.

The first successful machine design, nicknamed 'Mother', appeared in January 1916. The vehicles were labelled 'water tanks' to fool German spies, and the name 'tank' stuck.

Tanks were first used in battle on 15 September 1916, when the British general Sir Douglas Haig ordered them into action at Flers during the Battle of the Somme. The effect was stunning. A German journalist reported 'mysterious monsters were crawling towards them over the waters ... the monsters approached slowly ... nothing stopped them ... someone in the trenches said "the Devil is coming"'. However, the initial advantage of surprise was lost, as there were too few tanks and not enough back-up troops.

The first tanks had many disadvantages. The eight-man crews were poorly trained, and they had to work in noisy conditions, suffocating fumes and temperatures of up to 38 °C. The tanks could only move at around 4 miles per hour, and they were steered using a 'tail' at the back of the tank which was an easy target for shellfire.

Better tank designs were developed as the war dragged on. The Germans were slow to produce their own versions, because the first British tanks had so many drawbacks. However, they did build antitank ditches to defend themselves from tank attacks. The Allies used 100 tanks more successfully at the Battle of Cambrai in November 1917, but the tank did not contribute to breaking the stalemate in the war until August 1918.

Despite this lack of success, the earlier remark of Lord Kitchener, the British Secretary of State for War, that the new tank weapon was just a 'pretty, mechanical toy' was not justified. By the end of the war, the German commander General Erich von Ludendorff considered the tank to be the German army's most dangerous enemy.

>> Activities

1 What made life in the trenches so uncomfortable?

2 What happened when men went 'over the top'?

3 What impact did the development of poisonous gas and tanks have on trench warfare?

Propaganda

Men carried on fighting in the war despite the dreadful conditions. This was partly because people on both sides of the war were exposed to propaganda, or slanted information.

How was propaganda used in the war?

There was no public radio or television during the First World War, and most information was published in newspapers, which were censored by governments and military authorities. This censorship took various forms:

> Bad news was suppressed. For example, the German casualty figures for the Battle of the Marne were never published.

> The courage of the national armies was exaggerated. One Paris newspaper told its readers that 'our troops laugh at machine guns now ... nobody pays the slightest attention to them'.

> Each side portrayed its enemies as evil and brutal.

THE BELLS OF ANTWERP

The famous case of the 'martyred' clergymen of Antwerp in Belgium is a good example of how propaganda developed during the war.

> A newspaper in Cologne in Germany reported that, after the fall of Antwerp in August 1914, bells were rung in churches throughout Germany.

> The Parisian newspaper *Le Matin* reported that the clergy of Antwerp were forced by victorious German troops to ring their own church bells.

> In London, *The Times* newspaper reported that clergymen who had refused to ring their bells after the fall of Antwerp had been arrested.

> The Italian newspaper *Corriere della Sera* in Milan reported that Belgian priests had been sentenced to hard labour for refusing to ring their bells to celebrate the German victory.

> *Le Matin* reported that Belgian clergymen who had refused to ring their bells were tied upside down inside the bells and used as human clappers.

SOURCE A

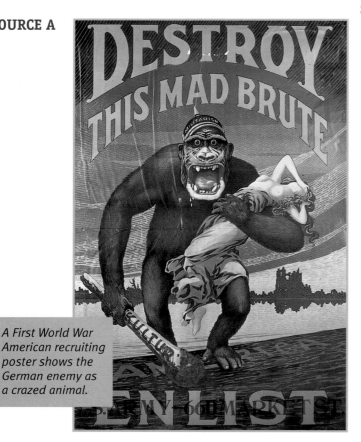

A First World War American recruiting poster shows the German enemy as a crazed animal.

SOURCE B

Germany defends her shores. The caption reads 'God punish England'.

SOURCE C

There were many accounts of atrocities, such as the following Canadian crucifixion story.

On May 15th, *The Times* reported ... during the battle at Ypres in April, troops had discovered the body of a Canadian soldier, crucified on a Belgian barn door, with German bayonets piercing his hands and feet. The story was almost certainly untrue but grew in the telling. Four days after the report in *The Times* a Canadian private wrote to his wife that it was not one but six Canadians who had been crucified. The next time the unit was in combat 'our officers told us to take no prisoners, shoot the bastards or bayonet them'. A bronze frieze exhibited in London showed German soldiers beneath the crucifix smoking and throwing dice.

Martin Gilbert, *The First World War,* 1994

SOURCE D

Another atrocity story described a 'German corpse factory'.

One such invention is the famous story of the 'German Corpse Factory', initiated in a report in London in *The Times* on 16th April 1917. This noted that 'one of the United States consuls, on leaving Germany in February, stated in Switzerland that the Germans were distilling glycerine from bodies of the dead'. This was followed by a report from a German correspondent about a 'Corpse Exploitation Establishment'. The author of this lie was probably Brigadier-General Sir John Charteris, head of British Military Intelligence. Some years after the war he admitted that he had produced the story, simply by switching the captions of two photographs: one showing Germans removing their dead for burial; the other showing horses' corpses on their way to a soap factory.

J. M. Winter, *The Experience of World War 1,* 1988

SOURCE E

This makeshift but powerful piece of propaganda was put up by the Coventry War Aims Committee.

>> Activity

What impact might these atrocity stories have had on people in Britain?

Fighting spirit

Conditions in the trenches were terrible in the war, and yet most British soldiers continued to obey their officers. Historians have suggested several reasons for most men doing as they were told.

Why did men carry on fighting in the war?

Did men fight in the hope of a better future?

SOURCE A

Hope was very important.

Men could not continue such a war without hope. The mirage of a better world glimmered beyond the shell pitted wastes and leafless stumps that had once been green fields and waving poplars. When every autumn people said the war could not last through another winter and every spring there was no end in sight, only the hope that out of it all, some good would come for mankind, kept men and nations fighting.

Barbara Tuchman, *August 1914,* 1962

SOURCE B

A postcard published during the First World War shows the idealised memory of home and family which kept many soldiers going through the appalling experience of fighting in the trenches.

Did men fight out of a sense of duty?

SOURCE C

Duty was a factor.

The vast majority of the men who served simply did what they were told to do. It was their duty, because the state said so; and thus the bloodbath continued for four years.

J. M. Winter, *The Experience of World War 1,* 1988

SOURCE D

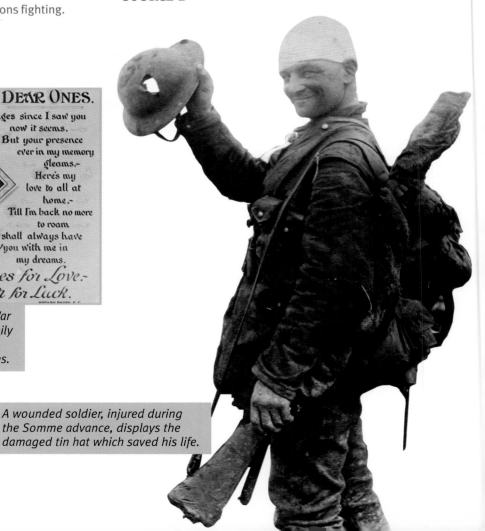

A wounded soldier, injured during the Somme advance, displays the damaged tin hat which saved his life.

SOURCE E

Cheerful One (to newcomer, on being asked what the trenches are like). "IF YER STANDS UP YER GET SNIPED; IF YER KEEPS DOWN YER GETS DROWNED; IF YER MOVES ABOUT YER GET SHELLED; AND IF YER STANDS STILL YER GETS COURT-MARTIALLED FOR FROST-BITE."

A difficult situation to smile about. Nevertheless, this Punch *cartoon shows a humorous response to the impossible situation which faced troops in the trenches.*

Did men fight because humour made the suffering bearable?

The British regiments produced field newspapers that contained jokes, stories and cartoons. Trenches were given humorous names and nicknames such as Sniper's Alley.

SOURCE F

Soldiers used black humour to keep up their morale, and they sang songs like this:

The Old Barbed Wire
If you want to find the old battalion
I know where they are
I know where they are
If you want to find the old battalion
I know where they are
They're hanging on the old barbed wire.

Did men fight because they were afraid of being shot?

British discipline was very strict during the First World War. Anyone who disobeyed orders or acted in a 'cowardly' way could find himself in very serious trouble. Thousands of troops were put on trial before a court martial (a special military court). If they were found guilty of cowardice, they were shot.

>> Activity

Why did the soldiers carry on fighting in the First World War?

Recruitment and resistance

At the start of the First World War, many thousands of British men volunteered to fight. Later, many were forced to fight. Some refused to take part in the war.

Why did people have different attitudes towards fighting?

SOURCE A

Daddy, what did YOU do in the Great War?

Recruiting posters used many different tactics to appeal to people's sense of duty.

During August 1914, thousands of young men flocked to join the British army. They were caught up in the patriotic enthusiasm of the time, and they wanted to share in the glory of the war, which everyone thought would be over by Christmas. Then, as the trench warfare in France and Belgium dragged on, the number of volunteers gradually fell. In January 1916, the British government introduced the *Military Service Act*, under which single men between 18 and 41 could be conscripted into, or made to join, the army. This measure was extended to married men in March 1916.

Some men believed that they should not be conscripted, and they had to appeal to a tribunal made up of military and local people to prove their case. Certain categories of men might be excused combatant (fighting) service:

> men who were physically unfit to serve in the armed forces

> men doing essential civilian jobs (such as miners, farmers and engine drivers)

> genuine conscientious objectors (people who would not fight for religious or moral reasons).

SOURCE B

Medical examinations were supposed to weed out recruits who were unfit for military service. In practice, the examinations were superficial and often passed men into the army who suffered from various illnesses.

Two kinds of bravery

Conchies

SOURCE C

Conscientious objectors preparing soil to grow crops on Dartmoor where they were imprisoned.

When conscription was introduced in Britain, about 16,000 men fell into the conscientious-objector category. They were known as 'conchies'. Just under half of these agreed to perform noncombatant service – that is, they helped with ambulance and stretcher work behind the lines. The remainder, who refused to do any army service at all, were conscripted into the army, and then court-martialled (tried before a military court) for refusing to obey an officer. A few of these men were shipped to France, but most were put in prison. If they talked to each other, they could be put in solitary confinement on a diet of bread and water. During the war, 69 conchies died in prison, and around 39 went insane.

Under-age volunteers

Many young men who joined the army between 1914 and 1916 were under the minimum age for military service. One of these boys was Valentine Strudwick, who came from Dorking in Surrey. Valentine was lazy, and he left school as soon as he could to do casual labouring work such as helping on farms and coal bagging. In January 1915, at the age of 14 years and 11 months, he ran away from home to join the army. He dropped his first name and called himself Joe, and his height helped him to get through the recruiting process.

SOURCE D

An article in a local newspaper takes up the story.

With only six weeks' training the lad was sent over to France. Within a short time he lost two of his chums who were standing near him. The shock was such, with the addition of being badly gassed, that he was sent home and was for three months in hospital in Sheerness. On recovering he rejoined his regiment in France.

Dorking and Leatherhead Advertiser, 22 January 1916

Valentine had been gassed. He had seen two of his best friends die, and spent three months in a hospital far from home. On his return to France, he was killed, aged just 15.

SOURCE E

A copy of The Boy's Own Paper *from October 1915 carries a patriotic cover and contains an article about British boys' work in wartime. Many under-age boys managed to hide their ages and volunteered for active service.*

>> Activities

1 Who were the conscientious objectors, and how were they treated?

2 What happened to Valentine Strudwick? Was his courage different from that of the conchies?

Verdun

A war of attrition

The Germans, French and British were all convinced that a breakthrough could only be achieved on the Western Front by wearing down the enemy with offensive after offensive (*offensive à outrance*). This kind of war is called a war of attrition. The generals believed that the side with the better morale (that is, confidence and discipline) and fighting spirit would win in the end, whatever the cost.

The accuracy of the artillery fire during the bombardment before the start of an offensive was critical. By 1916, the 'creeping barrage' system had been developed, in which the infantry advanced immediately after its artillery had shelled the next line of trenches. This method worked sometimes, but the advance could be interrupted by a gas attack, or by the artillery shelling their own soldiers by mistake.

Attack on Verdun

By the winter of 1915, after a year of stalemate, the German government was receiving reports from its spies that the French army was close to breaking point. The German commander General Von Falkenhayn believed that an offensive against the French at a vital part of the front line would force France to 'throw in every man they have – if they do so the forces of France will bleed to death'. This would knock the French out of the war, and force Britain to negotiate a peace.

French soldiers at Verdun.

Falkenhayn chose to attack Verdun, a major French fortress on the Western Front. He was not interested in whether he captured the system of forts or not. His aim was to kill as many French soldiers as possible and break the fighting spirit of the French army.

The Germans made their preparations for their offensive in great secrecy. Night transports moved 3 million shells to camouflaged dumps. On 21 February 1916, the preliminary German bombardment began: 850 guns poured 100,000 shells an hour for nine hours into the French defences along an 8 mile front. Shortly afterwards, 140,000 German foot soldiers crossed into no-man's land. The German attack was relentless, and the soldiers used gas shells and flame-throwers. The winter weather was dreadful, and it lasted for weeks.

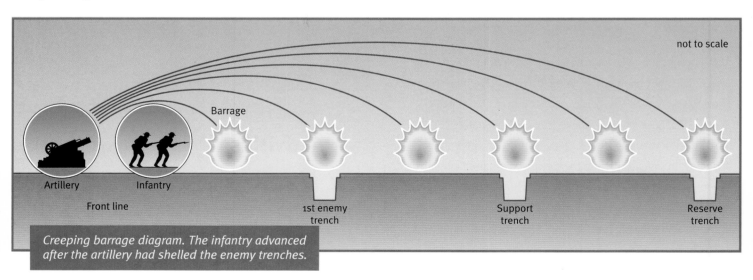

not to scale

Barrage

Artillery | Infantry

Front line

1st enemy trench

Support trench

Reserve trench

Creeping barrage diagram. The infantry advanced after the artillery had shelled the enemy trenches.

The Battle of Verdun

At first, the German bombardment and offensive seemed to be working. The French were pushed back, and Fort Douaumont (part of the Verdun complex) was captured in February. In the first five weeks of the offensive, one German soldier was killed every 45 seconds. However, as the French death rate was higher, the German high command reckoned that its own casualties were a fair price to pay.

Falkenhayn succeeded in provoking a political crisis in France. The French War Minister screamed at his generals: 'If you surrender Verdun, you will be cowards, cowards! If you abandon Verdun, I will sack you on the spot.' More worryingly still for France, some of its military units were on the brink of mutiny. It seemed that, despite the high German price tag, Falkenhayn's offensive might pay off.

Ruined houses in a suburb of Verdun.

General Pétain in 1916.

However, Falkenhayn met his match in the French general Philippe Pétain. On his appointment, Pétain immediately ordered his men to 'retake immediately any piece of land taken by the enemy'. The following day he issued his famous order: 'They shall not pass.' In addition to inspiring his men, Pétain realised how important good organisation was. He supervised a new supply line that poured 50,000 tonnes of stores and 90,000 men a week, in 6,000 trucks a day, to the Verdun defences. Mutineers were shown no mercy, and, in some units, one in every ten mutineers was shot.

By August 1916, the French were losing fewer men than the Germans. Falkenhayn tried to justify his offensive by claiming that ten French men had died for every five German deaths. His argument was rejected, and he was replaced by the Germans on 30 August. By November 1916, the French clearly had the upper hand. The reported figures vary, but it seems clear that there were around 700,000 casualties, of which some 362,000 were French and around 337,000 German.

Discussion point

> Which side won the Battle of Verdun?

Field Marshal Sir Douglas Haig

Field Marshal Sir Douglas Haig was Commander-in-Chief of the British armies in France from 1916 to 1918. He was in charge of the British forces at the Battle of the Somme, which was fought from July to November 1916. This was one of the bloodiest battles in the history of warfare.

Was Haig a hero, or the 'butcher of the Somme'?

SOURCE A

Field Marshal Sir Douglas Haig.

VIEWS OF HAIG

There are three main views of Haig and his handling of the Somme offensive of 1916.

> Haig was still the British Commander-in-Chief when the Allies finally achieved victory in the First World War in 1918. This proves that he was right to order the offensives that he did, including the one on the Somme.

> Haig deserves the title 'butcher of the Somme'. His incompetence and inflexibility made him personally responsible for the deaths of many thousands of men.

> Haig was the best man for the job at the time. The British casualties were no worse than those of the French and the Germans.

After the Battle of the Somme, Haig was treated like a hero. In December 1916, King George V appointed Haig to the rank of field marshal. After the war, Haig was made an earl and given £100,000 by Parliament. However, some historians have been very critical of his leadership.

While the battle for Verdun was at its height in spring 1916, the French and the British planned a major offensive on the Somme. The aim was to break through the German front line and take the pressure off the French defenders at Verdun. However, as the planning proceeded, the French cut down their contribution, and pressed for a mainly British offensive to take place in June 1916. Some historians claim that the British commander, Sir Douglas Haig, was put under political pressure to agree to the French demands.

> What can we learn about Haig from the way he prepared for the Battle of the Somme?

Was the offensive well planned?

Haig's plan was to order a 'big push' on the Somme front to create a gap in the German front line through which he would pour cavalry. If this was not successful, he would mount further infantry attacks to weaken the German front line and force the Germans to use up all their reserve forces. The cavalry would then be able to break through.

The British preparations

> Reports on British preparations for the offensive appeared in local French newspapers.

> The Germans on the Somme could see British ammunition dumps growing in size by the day.

> As was usual for senior commanding officers at the time, Haig directed the battle from well behind the front lines from his headquarters at a château in Querrieux.

> Haig planned to attack high ground that was well defended. The German commander Falkenhayn could not believe that any general would do this.

> The plan was that a British bombardment would destroy the German defences, kill all the German defenders, cut the barbed wire of the German defences, and leave the British infantry free to walk across no-man's land.

> The British captured a German concrete dugout a week before the attack. Despite the fact that they could see how well built and safe the German defences were, the British plans were not changed as a result.

> The British bombardment began on 24 June 1916; it was planned that it would last five days. 1,400 guns fired a barrage of 1.7 million shells. The bombardment was extended by two days as some of the shells were faulty.

SOURCE B

A British howitzer gun.

THE BRITISH PLAN IN THEORY

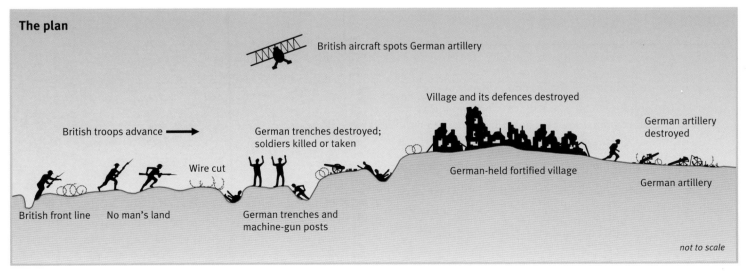

The plan

British aircraft spots German artillery

Village and its defences destroyed

German artillery destroyed

British troops advance →

German trenches destroyed; soldiers killed or taken

Wire cut

German-held fortified village

German artillery

British front line   No man's land

German trenches and machine-gun posts

not to scale

What went wrong on the first day of the Somme offensive?

THE BRITISH PLAN IN ACTION

The reality

Cloud prevented aircraft spotting artillery

Village destroyed, but defences intact

German artillery still firing

German trenches only partly destroyed, soldiers still fighting

British troops killed or wounded

Wire not cut

Germans sheltered in deep dug-outs until bombardment was over

not to scale

> By 1 July, the German barbed wire had not been cut by the British bombardment. A large number of the British shells had been faulty.

> At 07.30 a.m. on 1 July 1916, the British creeping barrage began, and British infantry went 'over the top'. The Germans came out of their safe underground dugouts to man their machine-gun posts. They were then able to mow down their slow-moving British opponents.

> The Germans were well-armed with thousands of American Lewis machine guns, which they had bought before the war started. Haig described these guns as 'a much overrated weapon' that could be captured by 'grit and determination'.

SOURCE C

George Coppard, a British machine gunner, remembered the battle.

How did the planners imagine that Tommies [British soldiers] would get through the German wire? Any Tommy could have told them that shell fire lifts wire up and drops it down, often in a worse tangle than before.

George Coppard, *With a Machine Gun to Cambrai*

SOURCE D

A German machine gunner described the first wave of the offensive.

The officers were in front. I noticed one of them walking calmly carrying a walking stick. When we started firing we just had to load and reload. They went down in their hundreds. You didn't have to aim, we just fired into them.

John Simkin, *Contemporary Accounts of the First World War*, 1981

The offensive carried on with ferocious fighting until it petered out in the dreadful weather of November 1916. There were around 620,000 British and French casualties, and 450,000 German casualties.

The land gained by the British was 7 miles deep at most. For the five months in 1916 during which the Battle of Verdun and the Battle of the Somme were being fought at the same time, 6,600 men were killed every day (277 per hour, and around 5 every minute).

SOURCE E

German dead, during the Battle of the Somme, October 1916.

> Look at the following sources, and decide which of the above views of Haig they support.

SOURCE I

The Harvest of Battle by C. R. W. Nevinson depicts a scene of death and devastation which was common on the Western Front.

SOURCE F

A Punch cartoon congratulates Haig as the conquering hero.

SOURCE G

The military historians Herwig and Heyman saw Haig like this:

He was unimaginative, he displayed an obstinacy in adhering to fixed plans regardless of the facts, even at the price of destroying his own armies.

John Laffin, *A Western Front Companion*, 1994

SOURCE H

This was another view of the Battle of the Somme:

The simple reason why the British Army had such heavy casualties between 1914–1918 was that it was doing far more fighting, against a very powerful foe, than it has ever done before or since. It would in fact have been a mistake if the British army had not had very heavy casualties in carrying out that task.

John Terraine, *The First World War*, 1965

SOURCE J

Haig's intelligence has been called into question.

The selection of leaders from pre-war professionals was likely to produce a rich crop of mediocrities. Put bluntly, the nobility and gentry used the army as a dumping ground for their stupid children.

Denis Winter, *Haig's Command – A Reassessment*, 1991

SOURCE K

Other historians have not been as critical of Haig.

Haig had to do what he did and though he did not succeed, no-one better was found to take his place.

A. J. P. Taylor, *The First World War*, 1963

>> Activities

1 Discuss which of the three views of Haig listed at the beginning of this investigation is the most accurate.

2 Explain your view of Haig in an essay, as follows:
   > Describe who Haig was and what he did.
   > Explain whether you agree that he was a hero.
   > Explain whether you agree with the view of him as the 'butcher of the Somme'.
   > Explain whether you agree that he 'did his best'.

Breaking the stalemate on the Western Front

The only way in which the stalemate on the Western Front could be broken was if one of the following occurred:

> The Schlieffen Plan had succeeded.

> One of the major offensives broke through the enemy front line and led to a massive defeat for the enemy.

> One or both sides were prepared to make peace.

> A breakdown in the morale of one of the armies led to its collapse and mutiny.

None of these things happened during the early years of the war.

During 1917, the British and the French launched fresh offensives against the German front line. At Passchendaele, near Ypres in Belgium, there were over 500,000 British casualties between July and November, for little gain. In April, in the new French offensive, there were 40,000 French casualties on the first day and 187,000 casualties before it was called off six weeks later. French soldiers mutinied, and the French launched no more new offensives on the Western Front. In the meantime, the Germans launched no offensives in 1916 or 1917. They actually withdrew from part of the front line to occupy more powerful defensive positions (the Siegfried Line) that they had built behind it. By 1918, each side had grown used to the stalemate on the Western Front, and few people expected a swift change.

Generals were far from the front; they followed rigid plans that allowed no freedom to officers at the front

The generals believed in a war of attrition. This meant wearing down the enemy regardless of the casualty figures, until their morale collapsed

Both sides wanted peace on their own terms

The morale of each army stayed high enough for the war to be continued

Why was there stalemate?

Technology was not advanced enough to lead to a breakthrough; gas, aircraft and tanks were not effective enough

No major breakthroughs could be made with the normal offensive methods: (a) the preliminary artillery bombardment always warned the enemy of an attack in advance; (b) mass attacks of infantry did not work

A French execution on the Western Front in 1917.

Discussion point

> Imagine that you are advising the British government and the French government in 1917. Explain what you believe is the best way of achieving victory on the Western Front.

The German offensives

In March 1918, Germany finally defeated Russia in the east. The Germans then took a final gamble to break the deadlock on the Western Front and win the war. They mounted an offensive code-named Operation Michael. On the night of 21 March 1918, on the Somme front, which was the weakest part of the Allied front line, the British were not expecting any German activity. There was thick fog, and there had been no German offensive for the last two years.

At 04.40 a.m., the Germans started firing several thousand guns at once along a 40-mile front, pouring high explosives and gas shells into the British front line for five hours. German engineers blew up explosives under the British front wire. The stunned British defenders faced, not waves of ordinary infantry at whom they could

German shock troops during the major German offensive, in June 1918.

fire as usual, but small groups of highly trained storm troopers armed with light machine guns, grenades and flame-throwers.

The weak British line was pushed back, and over the next few weeks the Germans advanced to within 35 miles of Paris. A gigantic German weapon, 'the Kaiser's Gun', shelled Paris every day. Kaiser Wilhelm II believed that the Germans had effectively won the war, but he was overconfident. By August 1918, the German push forward had failed, as a result of Allied reactions to the offensives and German weaknesses.

After their defeat at Amiens, the German politicians, soldiers and civilians stopped believing that they could win the war. Ludendorff described 8 August as 'the black day of the German army'. However, Operation Michael had broken the stalemate on the Western Front for good. After this, the outcome of the war was decided by troop movements, as in the early days of 1914.

Allied reactions	German weaknesses
The French general Ferdinand Foch was made Commander-in-Chief of the Allied forces in France. This improved the organisation of Allied forces	As in 1914, the German troops quickly became exhausted during the German advance
Because of the German offensives, American troops were rushed into action in France sooner than expected	As they moved behind the Allied front line, some German troops stopped advancing in order to loot French towns
The Germans were defeated at the Battle of Amiens on 8 August 1918 through the effective use of tanks	The German high command could not supply their forces with enough weapons and reinforcements to keep the advance going

Discussion point

> How did the Germans break the stalemate on the Western Front?

November 1918: the end of the war

The war in the west ended in November 1918.
The German government decided to make peace.

Why did the war end in November 1918?

Germany collapses

By late 1918, the German leaders and their people were divided about whether they should continue the war. The German leaders lost control inside their own country.

> In August, the Germans could not halt the Allied advance. The organisation of the German army was intact, but the troops were exhausted. They were suffering from low morale and a major flu epidemic, which weakened their ability to fight. Some German generals privately admitted that the German army could not face another winter of fighting.

> By October, Germany's allies Austria, Bulgaria and Turkey were crumbling from within.

> By the end of September, Hindenburg and Ludendorff had persuaded the Kaiser to appoint a new democratic government under Prince Max von Baden. This new government decided to negotiate an armistice, or ceasefire, with the Allies. Some historians think that the generals arranged for the new government to be set up so that it would take the blame for German defeat.

> In October, food shortages and low morale led to strikes and protests in German cities. Communists stirred up trouble in the hope of starting a Russian-style revolution.

> On 29 October, German sailors mutinied at Kiel in Germany and refused to fight.

> On 26 October, after a bitter row with the Kaiser, Ludendorff was dismissed. He escaped to Sweden, disguised in a wig and dark glasses.

> On 6 November, German communists seized power in the southern German city of Munich.

> Over 8–9 November, the German government was overthrown by a revolution. Prince Max von Baden handed over power to the socialist Friedrich Ebert. On 9 November, Germany became a republic. Under protest, the Kaiser and his family left for exile in the Netherlands, taking 40 carriages of the royal train packed full of treasures with them.

> On 11 November 1918, the armistice was signed, and at 11.00 the guns fell silent all over western Europe.

SOURCE A

German prisoners on the Western Front at the end of the war.

Germany loses the war

The Allies were taken aback by the speed of the German collapse. Field Marshal Haig muttered to a friend at the peace conference 'Why did we win?'. The Allied leaders and some Germans had been prepared for the fighting to continue into 1919. The answer to the question 'Why did Germany lose the war?' was vitally important, particularly during the years 1918–39.

WHY GERMANY LOST THE WAR

Theory 1. The Germans lost the war because the Allies succeeded in breaking the will of the German army and people to go on fighting. Credit should go to generals such as Field Marshal Sir Douglas Haig who wore down the morale of the German army against tremendous odds during the war years.

Theory 2. Germany lost the First World War because it was 'betrayed'. The German army was never defeated in battle. Revolutionaries inside Germany ended the war and 'stabbed the army in the back'. German generals at the time, and the German dictator Adolf Hitler later, used this as an excuse to blame democrats, revolutionaries, Jews and communists for the German defeat.

Theory 3. The Germans were defeated for several reasons. The offensive of March 1918 could have succeeded, but Ludendorff's planning was faulty. Once the offensive had failed, the German army was heading for defeat. Morale was also crumbling inside Germany. The new German government headed by Max von Baden decided to negotiate a compromise peace, with the idea of possibly restarting the war in the spring of 1919. The German revolution overthrew this government, and Germany became too weak to restart the war. Germany lost because of Ludendorff's failure and the collapse of fighting spirit inside the German army and among the German people.

SOURCE B

Celebration in London on Armistice Day, 11 November 1918.

>> **Activity**

Which of the theories about why Germany lost the war do you think is correct? Write one or two paragraphs to explain your theory of Germany's defeat.

The war on the Western Front

THE SCHLIEFFEN PLAN

Germany's prewar plan of battle, the Schlieffen Plan, failed within two months of the start of the war.

> Before the war, Germany believed that it would not be able to fight a war on two fronts against France in the west and Russia in the east.

> The German military planned to attack France by sending troops through neutral Belgium and taking Paris within six weeks.

> German troops would then be moved to the east to face the huge 'Russian steamroller' on the Eastern Front. This was called the Schlieffen Plan.

> In September 1914, the combined French and British armies halted the German advance before Paris at the Battle of the Marne.

> The exhausted Germans fell back, and dug trenches protected by machine guns to defend the land that they had occupied.

> The British and French then dug trenches opposite the German front line.

> By October 1914, the Schlieffen Plan had failed.

> By November 1914, the Western Front stretched from the North Sea coast of Belgium to the Alps on the French–Swiss border.

African troops wounded on the Western Front. Over 3 million troops from the British Empire fought to support Britain during the First World War. Soldiers came from countries including India, the West Indies, Africa, Australia, New Zealand, Canada and Ireland.

1914–18: STALEMATE

From late 1914 to early 1918, there was largely stalemate on the Western Front. The Germans and the Allies were evenly matched.

> Commanders such as Haig and Falkenhayn on both sides were committed to a war of attrition.

> The preliminary bombardments of each side failed to cut the enemy's barbed wire, and they warned the other side of an impending attack.

> Waves of attacking infantry were mown down by defending machine gunners.

> Neither side's artillery or infantry could breach the enemy's front line to let the cavalry through.

> The development of new technology, for example gas, tanks and aircraft, was not enough to break the stalemate.

> Despite heavy losses, little ground was gained by either side.

> Governments used propaganda and censorship to keep up morale. The soldiers fought on in the dreadful conditions out of a sense of duty and the hope that life would be better in the future. Discipline was harsh, and deserters could be shot.

> France and Germany used conscription throughout the war, and Britain introduced conscription in 1916, which kept up the supply of British soldiers. Conscientious objectors were treated harshly.

> Although there were mutinies in the French Army in 1917, the general morale on both sides remained strong enough to keep up the war effort.

> Neither side was prepared to compromise to make peace.

1918: THE BREAKING OF THE STALEMATE

The stalemate on the Western Front was finally broken in 1918.

> Using experienced troops released by the peace treaty with Russia, the German commanders Ludendorff and Hindenburg launched a surprise offensive on the Western Front in March 1918 with squads of highly mobile storm troopers.

> At first, the Allies had to retreat to within 35 miles of Paris.

> In August 1918, exhausted German soldiers who were relying on overstretched supply lines were pushed back by reorganised Allied forces. By then, these included the Americans.

> In November 1918, the German government was faced by the imminent defeat of its intact but demoralised armies on the Western Front and by revolution at home. It agreed to an armistice.

These two photographs show the village of Passchendaele from the air before and after the Third Battle of Ypres.

The war at sea

Control of the sea before the First World War

Since the British victory at Trafalgar in 1805, the Royal Navy had protected the sea lanes of the expanding British Empire. As an island nation, the British depended on their navy to protect Britain from invasion by sea and to guarantee the free movement of their traded goods. Any enemy would have to cut off Britain's sea-borne supplies of goods such as Canadian grain and Indian cotton if it wanted to starve Britain of war materials and food.

Britain's supremacy at sea lasted for nearly a century after Trafalgar before it was challenged. In 1898, Germany started to build its own modern fleet from scratch. The British responded to that challenge, and the 'naval race' began.

In 1904, the British admiral Sir John Fisher was shown a list of 154 ageing British warships. He responded by saying 'scrap the lot'. Fisher planned to modernise the British fleet to meet the German challenge, and he did this over the next eight years with ruthless drive and determination.

In February 1906, Fisher launched HMS *Dreadnought*, which had been built in a record year and a day. This was the largest, fastest, most powerful warship in the world, and all other warships immediately became outdated, including the ships of the Royal Navy. The race between Britain and Germany then intensified as each attempted to produce the highest number of the very expensive Dreadnoughts. By 1914, the British had won the naval race. Britain had by far the larger fleet, and it included 18 Dreadnoughts, as opposed to Germany's 13.

At the beginning of the war however, Vice-Admiral Reinhard Scheer of the German fleet said: 'When I consider my entire navy, I am forced to the belief that it is the equal of Britain's.' In spite of his confidence, the German surface fleet could make little impression on Britain's control of the seas early in the war. By December 1914, the British had destroyed all the squadrons of German warships sailing outside the North Sea, and they were blockading the German coast to prevent neutral ships from trading with Britain's enemies. German ships shelled resorts on the east coast of Britain, including Scarborough, but this did little damage, and the attacks were called off in January 1915.

The German fleet practising autumn manoeuvres in the North Sea, 1912. A torpedo boat cuts through a column of German warships.

The Battle of Jutland

Throughout the war, the British and German Dreadnoughts only fought each other once. On 31 May 1916, the two great fleets clashed at the Battle of Jutland. The map of the battle shows what a confused tangle it was.

Both sides claimed victory, but the result was actually a draw. The German fleet remained in port for the rest of the war. As a New York newspaper said: 'The German fleet has assaulted its jailer [the Royal Navy] but it is still in jail.'

The once-proud German fleet was surrendered to the Allies at the end of the war, and sent to the British naval base at Scapa Flow; the Germans sank their own ships there in January 1919 to keep them out of British hands.

Naval surface technology

The naval weapons of the future, the Dreadnoughts, were hardly ever used in the war, because they were too expensive to risk in battle. No Dreadnought was sunk, even at the Battle of Jutland. By 1922, Dreadnoughts were being used for target practice by the new warships of the British Royal Navy. As a result of the Battle of Jutland, set-piece battles using only warships became a thing of the past. Submarines and aircraft carriers were far more important in later years.

Discussion point

> What happened at the Battle of Jutland?

THE BATTLE OF JUTLAND

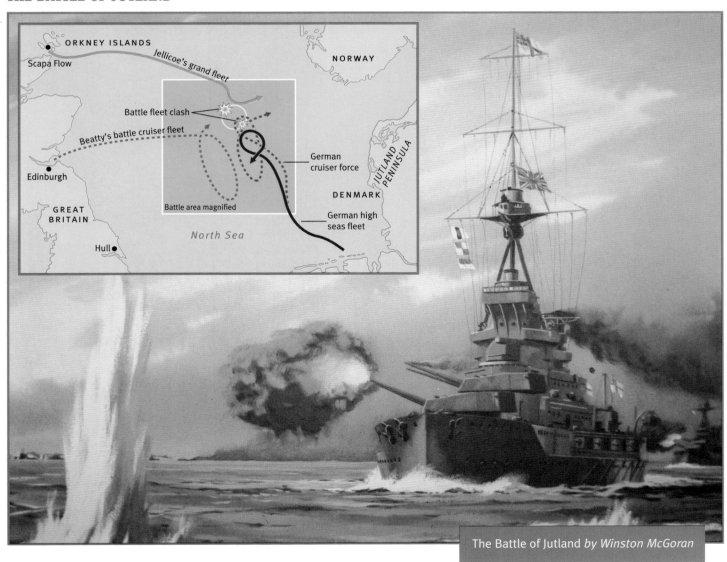

The Battle of Jutland *by Winston McGoran*

Submarine war

A new type of naval warfare developed during the First World War.
As the British controlled the surface of the sea, the Germans began
to use submarines to attack enemy ships.

How successful was German submarine warfare?

1915: the German submarine campaign

As its surface fleet was pinned down in port by the British Royal
Navy, the German government decided to use U-boat submarines
to sink without warning any neutral ships trading with Britain.
Up until this point, it had been the custom to signal to neutral
ships before sinking them, so that the sailors could leave the
ship first. This new form of combat was called 'unrestricted
submarine warfare'.

SOURCE A

German U-boat.

The sinking of the *Lusitania*

At noon on 7 May 1915, Captain Schweiger in the German
submarine *U20* sighted the British passenger liner *Lusitania* off the
coast of Ireland. Without issuing any warning, he fired a single
torpedo, which struck the ship and sank it in 18 minutes. The
Germans celebrated this act as their most successful achievement to
date in the war at sea.

SOURCE B

A recruiting poster issued shortly after the Lusitania *was sunk by a German submarine in 1915.*

The British were outraged by the sinking. There were around
2,000 passengers on board the *Lusitania* when she was hit; 1,198
drowned, including 128 Americans.

SOURCE C

A German newspaper claimed success.

The sinking of the giant English steamship is a success. With
joyful pride we contemplate this latest deed of our Navy. It will
not be the last.

Kölnische Volkszeitung, May 1915

Captain Schweiger of the *U20* claimed that he believed that the *Lusitania* was carrying war materials. He said that this was what must have caused the second massive explosion on the ship that followed the one caused by his torpedo. The German government stated: 'The *Lusitania* was naturally armed with guns — it is well known she had large quantities of war material in her cargo.'

Whether or not the *Lusitania* was actually carrying war materials is still disputed. One new theory claims that the second explosion witnessed by Captain Schweiger was caused when coal dust in the liner's coal bunkers exploded as the torpedo passed through the ship. Others claim to have discovered evidence that the *Lusitania* had munitions on board.

Whatever the real truth about the incident, the sinking of the *Lusitania* had a major impact in Britain, the USA and Germany.

> The British claimed that the Germans had ruthlessly sunk an unarmed passenger liner, sending innocent women and children to their deaths.

> The furious Americans protested to the German government, and some called for the USA to join Britain, France and Russia in the war.

> The Germans called a halt to unrestricted submarine warfare soon after the sinking.

At the start of the U-boat campaign, Germany tried to strangle British trade using only 21 submarines. By the end of 1915, 4% of British shipping and neutral ships trading with Britain had been sunk.

SOURCE D

This poster urges the British public to cut down on bread to preserve the stocks of wheat in the country.

1917: the second German submarine campaign

In February 1917, the German government once again began unrestricted submarine warfare. This time, the campaign was better prepared, and the Germans already had over 300 submarines in service. They were gambling on defeating Britain or forcing the British government to the peace table by cutting off the country's food supply. They were well aware that they were risking war with the USA as they had done in 1915, because their attacks on neutral ships trading with Britain included American vessels. However,

they thought that Britain would either come to terms with Germany or be defeated before American help could arrive in France.

The table of British shipping losses shows how successful the new U-boat campaign was. By April 1917, the British First Sea Lord, Lord Jellicoe, claimed there was only six weeks' food supply left in Britain.

1917	British ships sunk by U-boats
January	35
February	86
March	103
April	155

SOURCE E

The food-supply position was critical.

The margin of success was narrow. At one time there was less than a month's supply of wheat in England. The sinking of a single ship, laden with sugar, meant that jam-making had to be forbidden.

A. J. P. Taylor, *The First World War*, 1963

The U-boat campaign had two consequences

> Germany had expected the first outcome. On 6 April 1917, President Wilson of the USA declared war on Germany and its allies. However, this had little immediate effect on the war, because it was months before any trained American troops could arrive in France.

> The second result had not been expected. On the insistence of the British Prime Minister, David Lloyd George, the Royal Navy introduced a convoy system. From April 1917, merchant ships travelled in groups protected by warships, and they sailed in a zigzag pattern. This made it much more difficult to carry out an accurate torpedo attack on them, and far fewer British ships were sunk. In November 1918, the British losses were only 4% of British merchant ships.

British naval ships created a smokescreen

Destroyers and torpedo boats armed with weapons which could sink U-boats

Merchant ships were painted in camouflage

Zigzag sailing pattern to avoid torpedoes

The diagram shows the sailing pattern used by ships as part of the convoy system. The illustration shows a modern artist's impression of a U-boat which has surfaced to torpedo a merchant ship.

Technological advances at sea

Year	Naval technological changes	Political effects
1906	The Dreadnoughts are developed. This makes all other warships obsolete	The naval race between Germany and Britain is stepped up
1915	The British have surface control of the North Sea. Germany begins unrestricted submarine warfare	The sinking of the *Lusitania* nearly brings the USA into the war. The U-boat campaign is called off
1917	Germany restarts unrestricted U-boat warfare to starve Britain and bring it to the negotiating table	The USA declares war on Germany in April 1917
1917	Britain introduces the convoy system, which results in the failure of the U-boat campaign	By 1918, with its fleet permanently in port and the U-boats defeated, Germany has lost the war at sea

>> Activities

1 How successful was German unrestricted submarine warfare? Write an essay on this topic, and include the following points:

> Explain in a paragraph why the German government introduced this form of warfare.

> Discuss the U-boat campaign in 1915 in the first section of your essay, and assess how successful it was. Refer to quotations and facts about the sinking of the *Lusitania* and other relevant issues to support your arguments.

> In the second section of your essay, discuss the German U-boat campaign in 1917. Draw up two columns headed 'success' and 'failure'. Write down the successes and failures of the German campaign under the appropriate headings. Write up your evaluation using quotations and facts to support your argument.

> Write a conclusion that covers the following points. Could the 1915 German submarine campaign have succeeded? How close was Britain to defeat in 1917? Was it worth Germany risking war with the USA? Was it the fault of the German government that the U-boat campaign of 1917 did not defeat Britain?

2 What was the impact of technological change on the war at sea?

The British naval blockade of Germany

Throughout the First World War, the British Royal Navy mounted a blockade to prevent Germany from importing food and materials by sea. Historians still disagree about the amount of suffering that this caused, and the pressure that it placed on Germany to surrender.

How successful was the British blockade?

Many German civilians did go hungry during the war, but opinions vary as to whether this was because of the British naval blockade, or because of inefficient German management and bad weather.

Perhaps the greatest achievement of the blockade was that it caused unrest among the German sailors. Years of enforced idleness in harsh conditions created tensions between the German naval officers and ratings. One German sailor described his ship as 'an iron prison'. During the 'turnip winter' of 1916–17, aristocratic German officers feasted on good food and fine wine, while the sailors went hungry. German sailors mutinied in July 1917, and again more seriously in October and November 1918. Their revolutionary activity helped to topple the Kaiser and end the war.

SOURCE A

A food queue in Berlin in 1918.

SOURCE B

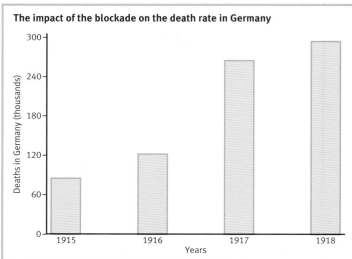

The impact of the blockade on the death rate in Germany

The effect of the Allied blockade on nutritional levels in Germany may be gauged from figures on increased civilian mortality. The food situation worsened after 1916, and hunger became rife. The worst period of the war was the summer of 1918, when severe food shortages coincided with the retreat of the main German armies.

SOURCE C

Some historians believe that the Germans brought their problems on themselves.

The Germans had already started the story that their food shortage was due to the British 'hunger blockade'. Yet Germany had not imported food before the war. The truth is that the Germans starved themselves. They took millions of men from the land for the armies. High prices encouraged the peasants to send their pigs and cattle to market. Then supplies ran short. 1916 saw a bad harvest, followed by a bitter winter. Turnips became the staple diet.

A. J. P. Taylor, *The First World War,* 1963

SOURCE D

Berliners at the end of 1918, scavenging through a rubbish heap, searching for food.

SOURCE E

Others believe that the Royal Navy played a major part in winning the war.

The Royal Navy provided the greatest contribution to victory by its perpetual and mainly unseen pressure ... the blockade's noose gradually tightened.

R. Hough, *The Great War at Sea 1914–1918,* 1982

SOURCE F

FOR NEUTRALS.

"Why do we torpedo passenger ships?"
Because we are being starved by the infamous English."

FOR NATIVES.

"Who says we are in distress?
Look what our splendid organisation is doing!"

This Punch *cartoon reflects the difficulty of deciding whether or not the British blockade inflicted suffering on German civilians.*

SOURCE G

There was disagreement about how badly the Germans were affected by the blockade.

Even the widely held view that the Germans had suffered severe food shortages was found hard to prove. President Wilson was told in a report dated December 1918 that food was plentiful in Germany ... an excellent harvest in 1918. German civilians had generally eaten better than civilians in the Allied countries, particularly away from the big towns.

Denis Winter, *Haig's Command – A Reassessment,* 1991

SOURCE H

This graphic contemporary picture by Louis Raemakers shows the Kaiser with the figures of War and Hunger, who are saying, 'Now you must accompany us to the end'. The Kaiser replies, 'Yes, to the end'.

>> Activities

Study the sources above and answer the following questions:

1 How bad did conditions get in Germany in 1914–18?

2 Can you tell whether these conditions were caused by the British naval blockade or German inefficiency? Explain your answer.

The war in the air

The First World War was the first major conflict in which aeroplanes and airships played a significant part.

How was the war in the air fought?

SOURCE A

The last fight of Captain Ball VC DSO MC, 17 May 1917 by N. G. Arnold.

Pilots and aircraft

The first aircraft were made of wood and canvas held together by wire. They had no radio, heating or navigational instruments, and the pilots had no parachutes. The pilots wore goggles and thick coats in cold weather, and rubbed whale oil into their faces to prevent frostbite. There were two types of aeroplane: biplanes had two fixed wings, one above the other, and triplanes had three. The aircraft had a top speed of 60 miles per hour.

To begin with, planes were used for scouting (spying on the enemy). Machine guns were fixed to fighter aircraft, and planes were used for bombing and attacking trenches. Both sides' propaganda glamorised pilots as 'air aces' to take people's minds off the grim slaughter in the trenches. The greatest First World War air ace was Baron Manfred von Richthofen, the 'Red Baron', who shot down 80 Allied aircraft before dying in battle.

Technology in the air

Machine guns were first mounted on planes in 1914, but the pilots were frustrated because they could not fire straight ahead without shooting off the plane's propeller. In 1915, the French pilot Garros invented a synchronised propeller system: a machine gun was mounted behind the propeller, and the bullets were fired between the blades as the propeller turned. However, the invention was so dangerous that metal plates had to be bolted onto the wooden propeller blades to prevent stray bullets from splintering them. Before his invention had been taken seriously by his fellow pilots, Garros was shot down.

The Germans captured his aircraft and copied his system. The German airforce was soon putting the synchronised system into all its planes, and the British and French then copied the system from the Germans. This is a typical example of how technology advanced quickly in the war, with neither side gaining a permanent advantage.

SOURCE B

Manfred von Richthofen, the Red Baron (centre), and the men of his pursuit squadron, known as the 'Richthofen squadron'. The Baron's brother, Lothar, stands behind him to his left.

SOURCE C

This magazine illustration from 1914 shows bombs being dropped by hand in the early part of the war.

Airships and bombing

In 1914, the Germans had a secret weapon which they planned to use to bomb British cities and break the morale of British civilians. This was a hydrogen-filled airship called a Zeppelin, which was 180 metres long. A manned gondola (cabin) and engine were suspended underneath the airship's frame. An observer could be lowered in a bucket to 800 metres below the gondola. During 20 Zeppelin raids on London in 1915, 188 civilians were killed.

SOURCE D

Zeppelin air raid on Southend, May 1915.

SOURCE E

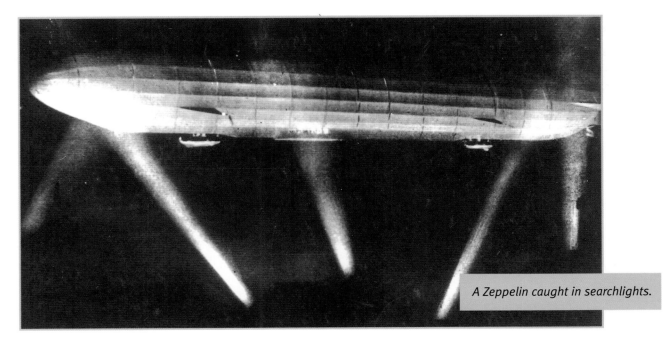

A Zeppelin caught in searchlights.

The failure of the Zeppelins

By 1917, the Germans had phased out Zeppelins, for the following reasons:

> The British had developed incendiary bullets which could puncture the skin of an airship and explode the highly flammable hydrogen inside.

> The British were using searchlights, night fighter planes and barrage (barrier) balloons to defend themselves against Zeppelin bombing raids.

> Too many Zeppelins had been lost because of bad weather and poor navigation. No parachutes were carried on the Zeppelins, and when one Zeppelin crew fell into the sea a British fishing trawler refused to rescue them.

SOURCE F

Death of a Zeppelin. Lieutenant Warneford's great exploit *by Gordon Crosby.*

By 1918, the British, the French and the Germans had all developed bomber aircraft that could damage enemy cities and kill civilians. Zeppelins had quickly become outdated, but they were the forerunners of the bombers of the Second World War.

Technological advances and their effects on fighting in the air

Year	Aircraft	Airships
1915	Garros invents the synchronised propeller system. The Germans develop the system after capturing his plane. The French and British copy it from captured German planes	Zeppelins raid British cities
1916	Fighter planes are developed to protect scout aircraft. The Germans start strafing trenches – that is, raking them with machine-gun fire from low-flying aircraft. They also start to fly in squadrons, or groups	The British develop incendiary bullets, and they use barrage balloons, night fighters and searchlights to defend themselves against the Zeppelins
1917/18	The British create the Royal Air Force as a separate service	The Germans switch to Gotha IV bomber planes for attacks on civilians, and the Allies develop bombers. Airships are no longer used in battle

>> Activities

1 Why did aircraft technology develop so quickly during the war?

2 Why could neither side in the war gain a permanent technological advantage in the air?

3 Why were Zeppelins unsuccessful in the long term?

The war at sea and in the air

THE SURFACE FLEETS

> In 1914, both the British Royal Navy and the German navy longed for a decisive sea battle.

> From 1914 to 1916, the British succeeded in clearing the seas of German ships and pinning the German navy down in port.

> When the British and German fleets did fight at the Battle of Jutland in the summer of 1916, neither side won a decisive victory. The British lost more ships, but the German fleet retreated to its base and stayed there until 1918.

> During the war, neither navy was prepared to risk losing a major battle (apart from at Jutland), especially as the cost of replacing Dreadnoughts would have been so high. A defeat could have meant losing the whole war.

THE GERMAN SUBMARINES

> In 1915, Germany engaged in unrestricted submarine warfare in and around British waters.

> The German sinking of the *Lusitania* in May 1915 nearly resulted in war with the USA. Shortly afterwards, the U-boat campaign was called off.

> In 1917, Germany mounted a second U-boat campaign designed to starve Britain and bring it to the peace table.

> This campaign was one of the reasons why the USA declared war on Germany in April 1917.

> The introduction of a shipping-convoy system by the British in April 1917 helped to defeat the German U-boats.

THE BRITISH NAVAL BLOCKADE

> A British naval blockade kept the German surface fleet in port for most of the war.

> The blockade contributed to food shortages in Germany, particularly towards the end of the war. This helped to lower German morale.

> The blockade enforced inactivity among the German surface fleet crews. It lowered their morale, and contributed to their revolutionary activity and mutiny in late 1918.

AIRCRAFT ON THE WESTERN FRONT

> In the early days of the war, aircraft were used for aerial scouting.

> Over the four years of the war, each side developed an airforce that included armed fighters and bombers.

> The rate of technological development in the air was the same on both sides.

> Although technical progress was rapid, the general effectiveness of aircraft remained limited. They were not powerful enough to bring about a breakthrough in the war.

Defending the realm

Almost as soon as the First World War began, the British government passed a new law: the *Defence of the Realm Act* (known as DORA). It set down rules for life in Britain during the war.

How successful was the *Defence of the Realm Act*?

The First World War was the first war in which the British government told British civilians that they were directly involved in the fighting. People started talking about fighting on the Home Front, which meant that they had to keep up morale in Britain, and send a constant supply of weapons, equipment and food to the Western Front.

On 8 August 1914, Parliament passed the *Defence of the Realm Act*, which was designed to regulate life on the Home Front. Additions to the Act were passed as the war progressed. DORA had four main objectives:

> to prevent people spying on British military and naval operations

> to protect Britain from the threat of foreign invasion

> to boost efficiency, particularly in the production of weapons and war materials

> to ensure that there was an adequate food supply for the British population.

Secrecy

DORA banned people from discussing the armed forces and their operations in public places or spreading rumours about them. Newspapers were censored. It was forbidden to use invisible ink when writing letters abroad.

Invasion threats

DORA banned the ringing of church bells in wartime unless Britain was invaded. The sale of binoculars was forbidden in case they were seized by invaders.

War production

DORA allowed the government to take over any factory or place of work for war production. Later laws included measures designed to lengthen hours of work and cut down on drinking by workers. Drunkenness was believed to be a major problem.

> The introduction of British Summer Time extended the hours of daylight during which work could be done.

> Pub opening hours were cut.

> It became illegal to buy rounds of drinks or to purchase whisky or brandy in railway refreshment stores.

> It became legal to water-down beer.

Despite these rules, the number of strikes increased, and the government was unable to stop production being lost as a result. However, by the end of the war, British industry had succeeded in improving the amount and quality of war materials reaching the British troops. This had been helped by the employment of women in the munitions factories, which manufactured weapons and ammunition.

SOURCE A

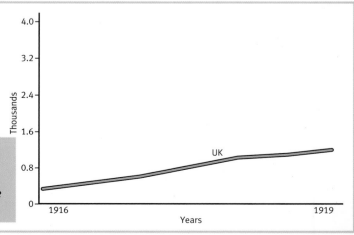

The increase in the number of strikes in the UK between 1916 and 1919 revealed the strain on the workforce from overwork and the sacrifices of war. The strike statistics tend to underestimate the scale of dissatisfaction because they leave out many unofficial strikes.

Food supplies

DORA made it illegal to feed bread to chickens, dogs and horses; even in 1914 there was an awareness that food should not be wasted. It was not until 1916 and 1917 that Britain was hit by serious food shortages. The government reacted to the U-boat campaign of 1917 by introducing voluntary rationing to cut down on food consumption.

People were supposed to eat no more than three-quarters of a pound (around 340 grams) of sugar, four pounds (around 1.8 kilograms) of bread, and two and a half pounds (around 1.1 kilograms) of meat each week. However, poor people could not afford to eat much sugar and meat in any case, and the rich continued to buy food illegally on the black market. The voluntary system therefore failed, and the food shortages continued.

Another DORA measure allowed the government to take over land that it needed. By 1917, public parks and other spare spaces were used for allotments where vegetables could be grown. 1.2 million hectares were ploughed up for farming between 1914 and 1918 in addition to the existing farmland. Thousands of women signed up for the Women's Land Army to help with farm work.

SOURCE B

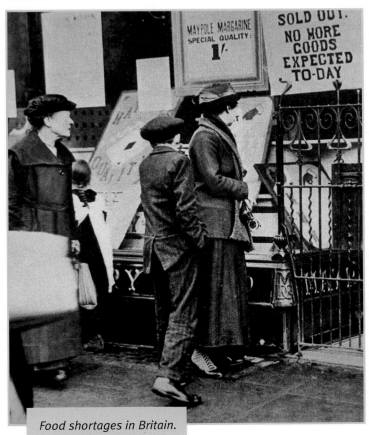

Food shortages in Britain.

SOURCE C

A Women's Land Army recruiting poster.

However, all this still did not produce enough food, and full-scale rationing was introduced in 1918. The rationing meant that ordinary people felt less resentful about the diet eaten by the rich, and it actually increased the amount of healthy food eaten by the poor. However, weakness caused by the generally poor diet during the war meant that people easily fell ill in the flu epidemic that swept Europe in 1918, which killed 228,000 war-weary Britons.

>> Activity

Imagine that you are writing a secret report for the British government in 1918. Assess the effectiveness of DORA, and make recommendations for improving the law in future wars.

The war and British women

The war had an impact on the way most women lived their lives. Historians argue about the way in which the lives of women in Britain were changed between 1914 and 1918.

What effect did the war have on British women?

The war changed the position of British women in society in every area: at work, in the family, personally, and politically.

Women's political rights

In 1914, Britain was a divided society. There were clear divisions between the upper class, the middle class and the working class. Most of society was controlled by men. A woman was supposed to be a good wife and mother, and her place was in the home. In fact, however, most working-class women had to work to help support their families. Women could not vote in elections, but some female activists (the suffragettes) had campaigned for years, sometimes using violence, for Parliament to give all women the right to vote.

SOURCE A

A woman munitions worker during the First World War.

At the outbreak of war in August 1914, most of the members of the suffragette movement enthusiastically supported the war effort. They saw this as a way of proving that women were worthy of the vote. Suffragettes such as the Honourable Evelina Haverfield united with former enemies such as the rich and powerful Duchess of Sutherland to form volunteer groups.

In 1915, the famous suffragette Mrs Pankhurst organised a march to encourage employers to take on more women in munitions factories. The costs of the march were paid by her former political enemy David Lloyd George, then the Minister of Munitions. By November 1915, the women's newspaper *Votes for Women* was appealing for votes for heroines as well as votes for heroes.

In November 1918, a change of public mood about this issue led to women over 30 being given the vote and the right to stand as Members of Parliament. Some historians believe that this would have happened eventually anyway, but the way in which women supported the war effort certainly helped to change male opinion.

SOURCE B

A prominent British politician spoke in Parliament about women's contribution to the war effort.

How could we have carried on the war without women? Wherever we turn we see them doing work which three years ago we would have regarded as being exclusively 'men's work'.

Herbert Asquith MP (former Prime Minister), speech in House of Commons, 1917

The image of women

During the war, the government at first exploited the traditional image of women as passive home makers. A popular song urged them to 'keep the home fires burning'. Recruitment campaigns encouraged women of all ages to use emotional blackmail to get their men to join the armed forces. Some patriotic women gave out white feathers (a symbol of cowardice) on street corners to young men who were not wearing a uniform.

SOURCE C

Women were encouraged to feel that they should push their men into joining the armed forces.

For nearly three years I have had a sweet-heart whom I love deeply. He is 25 and I 18. He is eligible for the army but has never offered ... Most of my girlfriends' sweethearts have gone and I feel horrid when I meet them with my boy: the humiliation is dreadful ... shall I give him up or not?

Letter to *Forget-me-Not* magazine, 26 June 1915

SOURCE D

Initially women were seen as playing a supportive role in encouraging their men to fight.

Initially, women who played an active role in the war effort, such as nurses, were portrayed as being loyal and supportive to men. The Germans helped to change this view. In 1915, the British volunteer nurse Edith Cavell was shot by the German occupying forces in Brussels in Belgium for helping Allied soldiers to escape. The image of British nurses changed overnight from that of 'ministering angel' to heroine.

It became more acceptable to see women in uniform, and fashion changed so that women could wear more comfortable and practical clothes. Attitudes towards women changed because of the number of different roles they were seen to play on the Home Front, and because of the way in which women ambulance drivers and nurses shared the suffering of the injured on the front line.

SOURCE E

V.A.D. stood for Voluntary Aid Detachment. Although the women shown in this poster were dressed as nurses, volunteers were recruited to do many different jobs as part of the war effort.

The way women lived

SOURCE F

The war changed the image of women for ever.

By 1918 the restrictive Victorian image of womanhood – physically frail, sheltered, leisured, private – had been undermined by the wartime experience of both sexes. It was now permissible for women to be physically courageous, enduring, responsible, conscientious, cheerful and outgoing.

D. Condell and J. Liddiard, Working for Victory? Images of Women in the First World War 1914–1918

Many new jobs became open to women because so many men were serving in the armed forces. Ordinary working-class women who did not volunteer to train as nurses or ambulance drivers at the front could do other categories of war work.

Category	Job
1	Some wives took over their husbands' jobs
2	Some did jobs that had traditionally not been done by women, for example driver or ticket inspector
3	Many produced munitions in arms factories

SOURCE G

British women working in a salvage depot.

SOURCE H

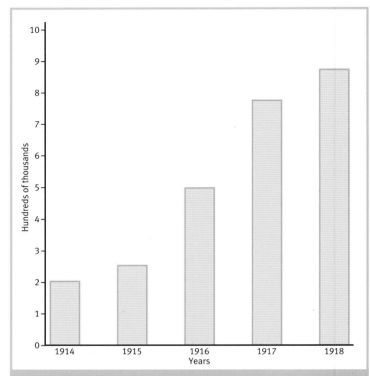

The number of women working in munitions steadily increased throughout the war.

By the end of the war, 900,000 women worked in munitions as 'munitionettes'. More women had jobs than before the war.

An extra 400,000 women had been employed as secretaries and clerks, and many had volunteered to join the Women's Land Army, which did farm work that had traditionally been reserved for men. Women's reactions to their new jobs depended on the woman's class, circumstances and personality.

WOMEN'S WAR WORK

'I already worked in this factory before the war, but in 1915 it changed to producing shells. I feel I'm doing my bit, but with my husband at the front, four children, and the house to tend to, I'm lonely and overworked.'

'I was so bored before the war. I couldn't even go out with a man without a chaperone. Now, as a land girl, I feel I'm doing my duty. We girls work like men, wear practical clothes and even smoke. It's hard work but great fun!'

'My sister and I were suffragettes before the war, but now we're nursing behind the front line in Belgium. Some awful sights we've seen have made us grow up fast, but this war has done a lot for women. Some of us smoke and drink, and we're sure to win the vote after the war is over. We just hope there are some men left to marry.'

Some of the ways in which the position of women improved during the war outlasted it, for example votes for women, more practical women's fashions, and (for middle-class and upper-class women) more freedom to drink and smoke and mix freely with other people.

However, many working-class women lost their hard-won status once the men returned in 1918. High unemployment closed many factories, and the men who did come home went back to their old jobs, replacing the women who had stood in for them. Even where men and women worked side by side doing the same jobs, women's pay was rarely equal to men's. One working-class man expressed his view of the situation in the workplace: 'Of all the 'orrible things this 'orrible war has done, these 'orrible women are the worst!'

Women of all classes had been brought up to believe that marriage and family life were their natural destiny, and perhaps the greatest blow to women was the death of hundreds of thousands of husbands, fiancés and boyfriends. In the 1920s and 1930s, a large number of women had to fend for themselves, with no prospect of ever getting married.

>> Activities

1 List the changes in the lives of British women that took place between 1914 and 1918.

2 List the ways in which life changed for
> working-class women
> middle-class women
> upper-class women.

To what extent did these changes improve life for each of these groups?

3 Which of the following statements most accurately describes the changes in the lives of women during the war?
> The First World War improved opportunities for all classes of British women.
> The First World War changed the lives of many British women, but not equally or always for the better.

The Home Front in Britain

THE *DEFENCE OF THE REALM ACT*

DORA changed the lives of ordinary British people during the First World War.

> DORA involved civilians in the war effort.

> British newspapers were censored.

> There were restrictions on pub opening hours.

> The government had powers to take over factories and organise industry for war production. Many factories switched to producing munitions, and they employed women workers.

> Extra land was ploughed up for farming in addition to the existing farmland. Members of the Women's Land Army did farm work. Public parks and other pieces of spare land were used for allotments.

> Food rationing was introduced in 1918 because of food shortages.

THE IMPACT OF THE WAR ON BRITISH WOMEN

> From 1914 to 1918, men went to fight at the front. This created new job opportunities for women.

> Some women took over their husband's job, or worked in the munitions factories as munitionettes.

> Others, particularly upper-class and middle-class women, worked as volunteer nurses and ambulance drivers in France and Belgium.

> The members of the Women's Land Army did farm work that had traditionally been reserved for men.

> More practical and comfortable women's fashions appeared in the war, and women began to have more social freedom, for example to smoke and drink.

> Women over 30 were given the vote in November 1918, partly as a result of women's contribution to the war effort.

> At the end of the war, many women lost their jobs to the

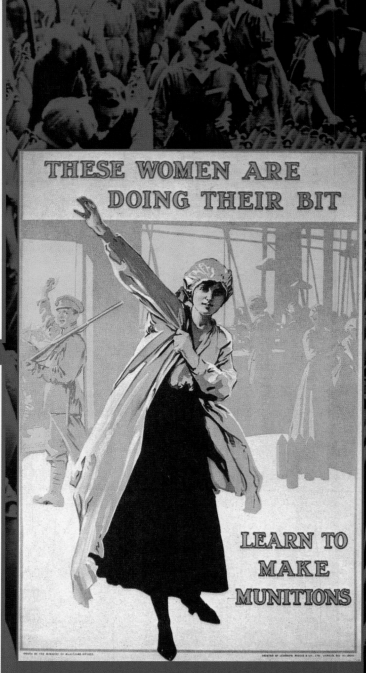

A poster recruiting women to learn to make munitions.

The Russian Front

The Central Powers did not just fight on the Western Front. They also had to struggle against Russian forces in the east. The war on the Eastern Front, between Germany and Austria-Hungary on one side and Russia on the other, had three important turning points: August 1914, June 1916 and March 1918.

August 1914: the Russian defeat

The Russian army was known as the 'Russian steamroller', and it was much feared by Germany. In August 1914, it invaded eastern Germany to take the pressure off the French and British forces on the Western Front. Despite its formidable reputation, the Russian army was poorly led and badly equipped. In some regiments, there was only one rifle for every ten men. The German commanders Hindenburg and Ludendorff were able to decode the secret Russian battle plans in advance.

This helped the German army to defeat the invaders heavily at two crucial battles in eastern Germany, at Tannenberg and the Masurian Lakes. In these two battles, the Germans took 135,000 Russian prisoners. The disgraced Russian commander committed suicide.

In his book, *The First World War*, the historian, A. J. P. Taylor, described the failure of the Russian attack on Germany:

> The Russian steamroller had been expected to carry all before it. In reality the Russians botched something up to aid their allies. The battle of Tannenberg cleared German territory for the duration of the war.
>
> A. J. P. Taylor, *The First World War*, 1963

The Russian army made better progress against Austria-Hungary, but by 1915 the cost of the earlier defeats had become clear. As the map of Europe in 1916 shows, the Russians had to defend an 800-mile front against continuous German advances.

THE RUSSIAN FRONT IN 1916

In 1915, the Tsar (emperor) of Russia, Nicholas II, took personal charge of the Russian army. His presence did little to improve the situation, and in 1916 it was left to General Alexei Brusilov to attempt to push back the German advance across eastern Europe with a surprise offensive.

Tsar Nicholas II.

June 1916: the Brusilov offensive

In the space of three weeks, the Russians made rapid progress, and they took around 250,000 prisoners. However, Brusilov had few troops in reserve, and eventually the Germans pushed the Russian advance back. What started as an outstanding Russian victory ended in another shattering Russian defeat. There were 1,000,000 Russian casualties in four months, which dealt a final blow to the morale of Russia's army.

Russian deserters continued to leave the front in huge numbers to get away from the brutal fighting conditions. By December 1916, 1,000,000 Russian soldiers had deserted from the army.

1918: the Treaty of Brest-Litovsk

In early 1917, Nicholas II was overthrown by a revolution in Russia. The new provisional government decided to continue the war effort, despite more Russian defeats, a hungry and war-weary population, and the opposition of the powerful Bolshevik revolutionary group (who were later to be called the communists). When the Bolshevik leader Lenin seized power in October 1917, he decided to make peace with Germany, at almost any price.

Germany and the Bolshevik government signed the Treaty of Brest-Litovsk in March 1918, and this marked the total defeat of Russia.

A Russian soldier forcing two of his deserting comrades back to the fighting.

The map of the outcome of the treaty shows that Germany gained a large amount of territory from Russia, and occupied a further vast area of land. Under the treaty, Russia lost a third of its wheat-producing areas and a quarter of its population, and had to pay war damages to Germany of 6,000 million deutschmarks.

After the armistice at the end of the First World War, the Treaty of Brest-Litovsk was annulled, but Russia still lost much of the territory covered by the treaty to Poland.

After the signing of the Treaty of Brest-Litovsk, Russia was out of the war. At the same time, American troops were beginning to arrive on the Western Front. After the end of the war in the east, the Germans were able to transfer crack German regiments from the Eastern Front to the Western Front for their surprise offensive in France.

Discussion point

> In the war on the Eastern Front, what happened at each of the turning points in August 1914, June 1916 and March 1918? Which of these points was the most important?

TREATY OF BREST-LITOVSK

Legend:
- Territory given to Germany
- Russian territory occupied by German troops

St Petersburg
Moscow
Brest-Litovsk
GERMANY
RUSSIA
UKRAINE
AUSTRIA

The Gallipoli Campaign

The Gallipoli Campaign was fought in 1915 by British, French, Australian and New Zealand troops against Turkey, which was an ally of Germany. The campaign ended in failure for the Allies. Historians have argued ever since about why the campaign was not successful.

Why was the Gallipoli Campaign a failure?

There are two main points of view about the importance of the Gallipoli Campaign.

SOURCE A

One view is that, if the Gallipoli Campaign had been successful, it would have broken the stalemate in the war.

Mr Churchill's idea was brilliant in conception. Our forces could have gone on to capture the Turkish capital, support Russia and change the whole course of the war. Poor planning and bad leadership on the Allied side spoiled all this.

Adapted from C. R. Nevinson, *The Dardanelles Campaign*, 1918

SOURCE B

The other view is that, even if the attack on Gallipoli had succeeded, it would not have made any difference to the overall course of the war.

It is of course interesting to guess what might have happened if Gallipoli had succeeded. It is my belief that it would have done little to help the Russians or halt the German victories on the Eastern Front.

Adapted from Robert Rhodes James, *Gallipoli*, 1965

The reason for the campaign

By early 1915, there was disagreement in the British government about the best way to defeat Germany. Some ministers and generals hoped that there would soon be a breakthrough on the Western Front. They were called the 'Westerners'. Other ministers and generals, the 'Easterners', believed that the Allies could win an easier victory by attacking Turkey. Turkey was Germany's weakest ally, and it was known as the 'soft underbelly of Europe'. The Easterners wanted to capture the Dardanelles, which were the straits, or sea passage, that protected the Turkish capital of Constantinople (now known as Istanbul).

EUROPE AND CONSTANTINOPLE

SOURCE C

Some members of the British government believed that an attack on Turkey could help the Allies win the war more quickly.

Lord Kitchener: 'The Dardanelles appeared to be the most suitable objective ... if successful it [the attack] would re-establish communication with Russia, draw in Greece and perhaps Bulgaria and Romania [as allies] and release wheat and shipping now locked up in the Black Sea.'

Lieutenant Colonel Hankey: 'It would give us the Danube ... for an army penetrating into the heart of Austria.'

Extracts from the notes of a British War Council meeting, 8 January 1915

The naval attack

In the first Allied plan for capturing the Dardanelles, the British and French navies were to attack the straits, supported by an Allied army. Because of the influence of the Westerners in the British government, the best British ships were kept in the North Sea, and the most experienced British troops stayed on the Western Front. The military force that was supposed to occupy the Dardanelles after the successful naval attack included Australians and New Zealanders who had never seen action before. When asked if they were up to the job, Lord Kitchener replied that 'they were quite good enough if a cruise in the Sea of Marmara was what was contemplated'.

The Allied navies, led by the British admiral Sir John de Robeck, began the naval attack in February 1915. Twenty-three Allied ships attacked the straits. British marines landed and spiked Turkish guns. Heavy Turkish gunfire forced an Allied withdrawal and the Turks laid mines across the Dardanelles. By March, British minesweepers had cleared most of the Turkish mines. The naval attack was nearly successful, but three Allied ships were sunk by stray mines, and three were badly damaged. Admiral Robeck called off the attack to prevent further losses, even though the lost ships were soon to be scrapped in any case. The Allies did not know that the Turks were down to their last line of mines, and that the Turkish gunners had run out of ammunition. The gunners deserted their posts on the tops of the cliffs. Only when the Allied ships had been sunk did they return to their guns.

The military campaign

After the Allied navies had failed to take the Dardanelles, it was decided that Allied support troops would attack the Turkish positions on either side of the straits. Raw British recruits were sent from Egypt to help in the attack. Only the British marines had seen action before.

The supplies for the Allied attack were loaded incorrectly in Egypt, and the supply ships had to be sent back to Egypt to be reloaded. This took another month. Turkish spies in Egypt reported to the German commander at the Dardanelles, Otto Liman von Sanders, that supplies were being packed for an Allied attack. The Allies' element of surprise was lost. Sanders then ordered reinforcements for the Turkish gun positions at the Dardanelles.

Lord Kitchener placed the inexperienced General Sir Ian Hamilton in charge of the military attack. Hamilton had no up-to-date maps of the area, and his information about the Turkish positions dated from 1906.

SOURCE D

Hamilton was not properly prepared for the attack.

Only two weeks before the attack, General Sir Ian Hamilton, classical scholar and poet, still had no plan of attack, no military staff, no accurate maps or charts, no knowledge of the enemy and nowhere to land his 73,000 men.

A. J. P. Taylor, *The First World War*, 1963

THE GALLIPOLI CAMPAIGN 1915–16

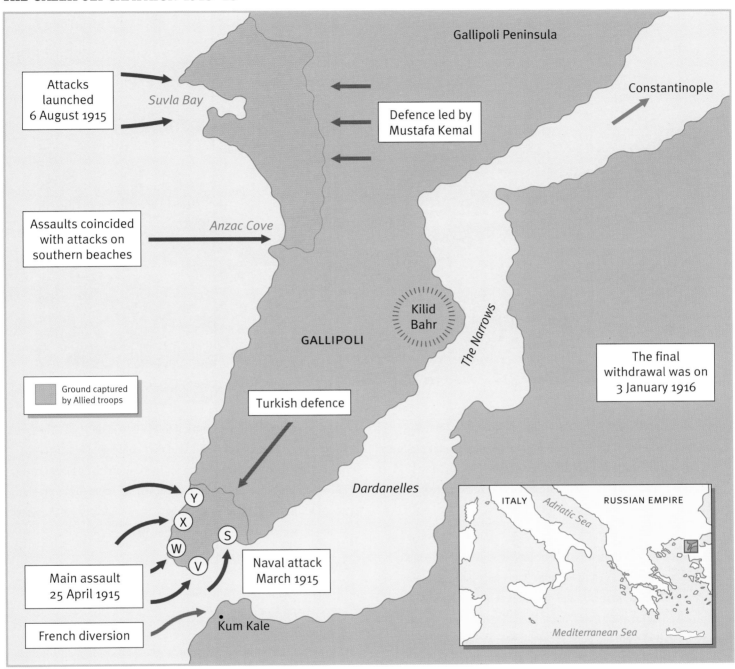

Gallipoli Peninsula

Attacks launched 6 August 1915

Suvla Bay

Defence led by Mustafa Kemal

Constantinople

Assaults coincided with attacks on southern beaches

Anzac Cove

Kilid Bahr

GALLIPOLI

The Narrows

The final withdrawal was on 3 January 1916

Ground captured by Allied troops

Turkish defence

Dardanelles

Y

X

S

W

V

Naval attack March 1915

Main assault 25 April 1915

French diversion

•Kum Kale

ITALY *Adriatic Sea* RUSSIAN EMPIRE

Mediterranean Sea

On 25 April 1915, Allied forces attacked at the points S, W, V, X and Y shown on the map of the Gallipoli Campaign. General Sir Ian Hamilton commanded the operation from the Greek island of Imbros, 15 miles away. The British troops on beaches X, W and V met with strong resistance. The attack on beaches S and Y was unopposed. The troops dug trenches on beach Y, but then withdrew because of an incorrect order.

At 4.30 in the morning, three parties of Anzac troops (Australians and New Zealanders) were dropped off from battleships in boats that each held 500 men. A strong current carried the boats 1 mile north to the base of cliffs. The troops met little opposition, but they became scattered, and they found it difficult to move forward across the rough ground.

SOURCE E

The Anzac landing, 25 April 1915, *by Charles Dixon*.

Just as on the Western Front, the Allies and the Turks then dug trenches, and wasted the lives of thousands of men in making brave but unsuccessful attacks on each other's front lines. In May 1915, 40,000 Turks attacked the Anzacs, and 10,000 Turks were killed in one day.

The Allied military engineers were unable to build piers and jetties at Gallipoli so that supplies could be landed quickly. The Allied troops soon ran short of ammunition. They only had six trench mortars, and there were no hand grenades at all. Soldiers improvised by creating home-made grenades out of empty food cans. Six out of eight big guns in the support artillery had broken down by August 1915.

The Suvla Bay attack

Hamilton planned to reinforce his battle-hardened troops by landing raw British recruits at Suvla Bay on 6 August. He asked for an experienced commander, but he was given General Stopford, who had never seen wartime action before. Stopford's last military command had been that of Lieutenant-Commander of the Tower of London. When Hamilton pressed for a better general, he was told that no one could be spared from the Western Front.

Stopford landed his raw recruits at Suvla Bay in the dark. The various units became confused, and they could not identify each other. They then sat on the beach for two days with no clear orders. The water tankers that had been anchored off-shore to supply the troops with water had no hoses, and so they could not get the water to the soldiers on the beach.

SOURCE F

The Allies did not advance immediately after their successful landing.

Stopford was in command. He did not go ashore. Instead he congratulated the men on their successful landing and settled down to his afternoon nap. They went off to bathe with no Turks between them and victory.

A. J. P. Taylor, *The First World War,* 1963

SOURCE G

Stopford left his men on the beaches for two days without water.

Parched men cannot swallow salt! Saltless, dehydrated, they reel on the edge of sunstroke and cannot march.

George Bruce, *The British Empire,* 1971

SOURCE H

Rear-Admiral Wemyss, who had taken over from Admiral Robeck as the commander of the British naval forces at Gallipoli, was appalled at the way in which the attack was handled.

The slipshod [careless] manner in which the troops had been sent out from England is something awful.

Rear-Admiral Wester Wemyss, 1915

By the time that Stopford's men moved forwards, the Turks were ready to resist them. The British captured little ground.

Eventually, in November 1915, the Gallipoli Campaign was called off, by which time there had been 16,000 cases of frostbite among the Allied troops.

SOURCE I

Preparing for the final evacuation of Allied troops from Gallipoli, which took place in January 1916.

The casualties

The British War Office had estimated that there would be 5,000 Allied casualties during the whole campaign, but the Anzacs lost 6,500 men in the first week alone. Over the whole campaign, the total of the casualties on both sides was around 500,000.

Many of the wounded died while lying on the beaches in queues for the hospital ships. One supply ship left Egypt with a cargo of mules and a vet in attendance. On its return journey, only the vet was available to tend the hundreds of wounded being transported to safety.

The Gallipoli Campaign is still remembered in Australia and New Zealand on Anzac Day, which celebrates the bravery of Anzac soldiers. Since Gallipoli, many people, including Anzac soldiers, have attacked British incompetence during the campaign. Hamilton and Stopford did not see action in the war again. Winston Churchill, who was one of the men behind the idea of the campaign, resigned from the British government.

>> Activities

How fair are the criticisms of the British leadership of the Gallipoli Campaign?

1 Did the Gallipoli Campaign have clear aims from the start?

2 Why did the Allied attack on 25 April fail?

3 Why did the Allied attack on Suvla Bay on 6 August fail?

4 Look at the statements of the historians in the first two sources, and explain which one you agree with most. Consider the idea behind the Gallipoli Campaign, the failure of the naval attack, and the military planning and leadership.

The other fronts

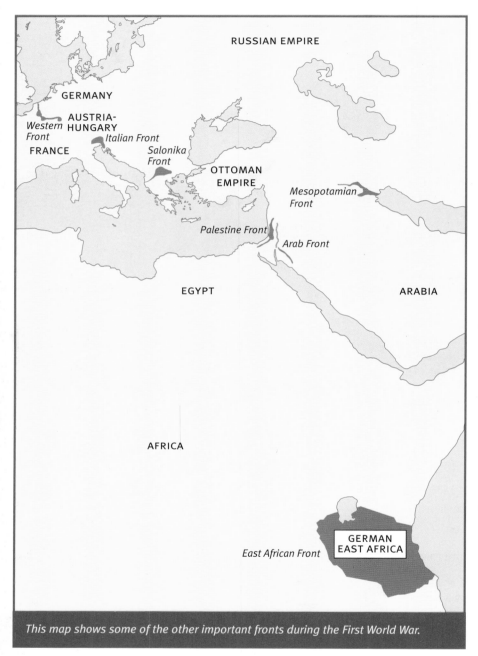

This map shows some of the other important fronts during the First World War.

The Salonika Front

In 1915 Bulgaria joined Germany as an ally and the British and French decided to open a front against this new enemy at Salonika in northern Greece. The frontline troops became known as 'the forgotten army' and little progress was made until 1918.

The Palestine Front and the Arab Revolt

In 1916 the British launched two unsuccessful attacks on Turkish-held Palestine from their bases in Egypt. In 1917 General Allenby led a more successful offensive which captured Jerusalem in December that year. The Turks were decisively defeated in 1918, a process helped by an Arab revolt against their rule. This was partly stirred up by a British agent, T. E. Lawrence, who came to be known as Lawrence of Arabia.

The Mesopotamia Campaign

In 1916 British forces landed in Mesopotamia to occupy this Turkish province and encourage the local Arabs to revolt. Instead the British were defeated and had to surrender after a disastrous siege at Kut. A further invasion in 1917 led to the fall of Baghdad and contributed to Turkish defeat in the following year.

The East Africa Campaign

All four German colonies in Africa were captured by the Allies during the war. Although German East Africa was invaded by the Allies, the German commander, General von Lettow-Vorbeck, fought a skilful guerrilla campaign. Using a small force of African troops, he did not surrender until after the war in Europe had ended.

Discussion point

> Look at the information on each of the fronts. For each one work out whether Britain and her allies were successful in this area.

The Italian Front

Italy, originally a member of the Triple Alliance, remained neutral through 1914 but was attracted into the war in 1915 by secret Allied offers of land at Austria's expense. From 1915 to 1917 the Italians fought a desperately hard campaign along their Austrian border before suffering a disastrous defeat at Caporetto in October 1917. British and French troops were rushed to reinforce the Italians who won an important victory over the Austrians at Vittorio Veneto in 1918.

The fighting on the other fronts

THE RUSSIAN FRONT

> In 1914, the German generals Hindenburg and Ludendorff easily defeated the Russian army at Tannenberg and the Masurian Lakes.

> Throughout 1915, Russian forces were pushed back by German advances along the 800-mile long Eastern Front.

> In June 1916, Brusilov mounted a spectacular Russian offensive. This was successful at first, but it eventually resulted in a crushing Russian defeat and 1,000,000 Russian casualties.

> In 1917, there were two revolutions in Russia. The Russian people did not want to carry on fighting in the war.

> In March 1918, Lenin's Bolshevik government agreed to the humiliating Treaty of Brest-Litovsk. The German troops on the Eastern Front were then moved to the Western Front.

THE GALLIPOLI CAMPAIGN

> In early 1915, some members of the British government believed that an attack on Germany's ally Turkey could help the Allies win the war. They wanted to capture the Dardanelles by landing at Gallipoli.

> However, the weakness of these Easterners meant that the plans and resources for the Gallipoli Campaign were never as good as those for the forces on the Western Front.

> An Allied naval assault was mounted at Gallipoli, but this failed.

> Allied military attacks on the Turkish positions were then badly planned and poorly carried out by the incompetent British commanders Hamilton and Stopford.

> The Allied forces and the Turks dug in for weeks of pointless trench warfare.

> Over the whole campaign, the total of the casualties on both sides was around 500,000. At the end of 1915, the Allies had to give up the Gallipoli Campaign and withdraw.

THE OTHER FRONTS

> The Italian army was not prepared for war when Italy joined the Allies in 1915.

> The Italians were worn down by fighting Austria-Hungary, which defeated them badly at Caporetto in 1917.

> The British and the French sent reinforcements and helped to reorganise the Italian forces. In late 1918, the Italians won a significant victory at Vittorio Veneto.

> The Allies opened up a front based at Salonika in northern Greece to fight the Bulgarians. This front was not seen as important by the Allies.

> Advances by Allied forces into the Turkish territories of Palestine and Mesopotamia met with mixed success. However, the campaigns contributed to the defeat of Turkey in 1918.

Index